Achieving Better Service Delivery Through Decentralization in Ethiopia

Marito Garcia
Andrew Sunil Rajkumar

Africa Region Human Development Department

THE WORLD BANK
Washington, D.C.

World Bank Working Papers are published to communicate the results of the Bank's work to the development community with the least possible delay. The manuscript of this paper therefore has not been prepared in accordance with the procedures appropriate to formally-edited texts. Some sources cited in this paper may be informal documents that are not readily available.

ISBN-13: 978-0-8213-7382-8
eISBN: 978-0-8213-7383-5
ISSN: 1726-5878   DOI: 10.1596/978-0-8213-7382-8

Marito Garcia is a Lead Economist in the Africa Region Human Development Department of the World Bank. Andrew Sunil Rajkumar is an Economist in the same department.

Library of Congress Cataloging-in-Publication Data has been requested

Contents

LIST OF FIGURES

LIST OF BOXES

Foreword

Over the last 10 years, several African countries have made notable progress in meeting the Millenium Development Goals (MDGs). Among them is Ethiopia where in 2005 nearly 75 percent of children enrolled in primary schools, a result of an impressive 9 percent annual growth in enrollment since 1993. Other indicators also registered improvements: immunization coverage for measles rose to 57 percent in 2005 from 40 percent in 1995. The percentage of Ethiopians with access to clean water rose from 19 percent in 1995 to 36 percent in 2005.

These improvements happened at a time of massive decentralization in Ethiopia—first from the federal to region, and subsequently into *woredas* (districts). This work presents an account of how decentralization has supported the delivery of basic services, including education and health to *woredas*. Because the authors were able to piece together detailed fiscal data from federal, region and *woreda* levels, as well as education and health data before and after the decentralization, the results provided insights into what has gone into the decisionmaking processes that contributed to the outcomes particularly in the education sector. It provides a glimpse of how the fiscal and administrative autonomy responds to the needs of their constituencies to improve service delivery.

This work provides evidence to the observation that the devolution of power and resources from the federal and regional governments to the *woredas* contributed to improvements in the delivery of basic services particularly in education. The independent surveys of beneficiaries by NGO groups in Ethiopia, perceive the service coverage and quality to have improved, especially in education. One of the most important results provided by the authors is that the decentralization has disproportionately favored the more remote *woredas*, the food insecure and pastoral *woredas*. This is a very important finding from a strategic standpoint because it indicates that decentralization itself is pro-poor, and helps those lagging areas in the country. The aggregate *woreda* spending for education for pastoral *woredas* increased dramatically with decentralization, faster than other *woredas*. Education budgets in food insecure woredas rose much higher than in food secure *woredas*, and narrowing the gap in educational outcomes.

Surely decentralization is only one among many other factors that contributed to the improvement in service delivery in Ethiopia. This work has also documented the changes in sectoral policies, for example the policy of using local languages at the lower primary level which improved school participation. Likewise, the growing role of communities, parent-teachers' associations (PTAs), and other local organizations, may have also contributed to better service delivery.

In preparing this volume the authors worked extensively with national experts and scholars not only from the capital city but also with regional specialists. This provided ample opportunities for both learning and capacity building for analytical work in this area, to understand the impact of decentralized service delivery on the population. Such capacity will no doubt support future work to help finely tune the decentralization processes, and improve the ability to find solutions to improve service delivery in a decentralized system.

Yaw Ansu
Director, Human Development Department
Africa Region
The World Bank

Acknowledgments

This book expands on a report prepared for the World Bank Africa Region's Human Development Department under the general guidance of Laura Frigenti (Sector Manager, AFTH3), Ishac Diwan (Country Director, AFC06), Yaw Ansu (Sector Director, AFTHD) and Trina Haque (Lead Economist, AFTH3). The book benefited from the analyses and reports of Jemal Mohammed Omer (AFTP2), Andrew Dabalen (ECSPE), Mirafe Marcos (SASPR) and consultants Mohammed Mussa, Gizaw Molla, Yigremew Adal, Jean-Paul Faguet, Nada Eissa, Mike Ingram, Tor Halvorsen, Robert Langley Smith, Mammo Kebede, Rahel Kassahun, Ephraim Kebede, and Caroline Pöschl.

The Ethiopia Human Development country team led by Trina Haque, and comprised of Getahun Gebru, Gary Theisen, Endashaw Tadesse, William Wiseman, Dr. Gebreselassie Okubaghzi, and Harold Alderman provided useful comments and insights throughout.

The authors are grateful for the invaluable comments received from the Ethiopia country team. In particular, they would like to thank Jeni Klugman, Anwar Bach-Baouab, Mesfin Girma Bezagawaw, Jemal Omer, Christine Lao Pena, and Agnes Soucat.

The book has benefited from comments by the peer reviewers Shantayanan Devarajan (Chief Economist, SASVP) and Elizabeth King (Sector Manager, DECRG).

The authors would like to express their special appreciation and gratitude to Woizerit Samia of the Central Statistical Authority, Ministry of Finance and Economic Development, and her team for facilitating access to data. Likewise, thanks are due to the Bureau of Finance and Economic Development as well as the Bureaus of Education, Health and Capacity Building of the regional governments of SNNPR and Oromiya for their assistance in obtaining data for this book.

Acronyms and Abbreviations

AED	Academy for Education Development
ATS	Average Teacher Salary
BA	Bachelors of Arts
BESO	Basic Education Strategic Objective
BOFED	Bureau of Finance and Economic Development
CSAP	Community School Activity Program
CGPP	Community Government Partnership Program
DPT 3	Diphtheria, Pertussis, Tetanus—3 doses of vaccines
FDR	Four Main Decentralization Regions
FSP	Food Security Program
FY	Fiscal Year
GER	Gross Enrollment Rate
GDP	Gross Domestic Product
GOE	Government of Ethiopia
HICES	Household Income and Consumption Expenditure Survey
HIV/AIDS	Human Immunodeficiency Virus/Acquired Immunodeficiency Syndrome
IMCI	Integrated Management of Childhood Illnesses
JRM	Joint Review Mission
MA	Masters of Arts
MDGs	Millennium Development Goals
MEFF	Macroeconomic and Fiscal Framework
MoFED	Ministry of Finance and Economic Development
NGO	Non-governmental Organization
PANE	Poverty Action Network of Ethiopia
PEPs	Public Expenditure Programs
PSCAP	Public Sector Capacity Project
PSNP	Productivity Safety Nets Program
PTA	Parent-Teacher Association
PTR	Pupil-Teacher Ratio
SDPRP	Sustainable Development and Poverty Reduction Program
SNNPR	Southern Nations, Nationalities and Peoples Region
SPG	Special Purpose Grant
UNICEF	United Nations Children Fund
USAID	United States Agency for International Development
WLI	World Learning Incorporated
WOFED	*Woreda* Office of Finance and Economic Development

Executive Summary

Ethiopia has made major strides in improving its human development indicators in the past 15 years, achieving significant increases in the coverage of basic education and health services in a short period of time. Improvements took place during a period of massive decentralization of fiscal resources, to the regions in 1994 and to *woredas* in 2002/03.

Decentralization Appears to Have Contributed to Improved Service Delivery . . .

The devolution of power and resources from the federal and regional governments to *woredas* appears to have improved the delivery of basic services. This is clearly shown in the Southern Nations, Nationalities and Peoples Region (SNNPR) and to a lesser degree in the Oromiya Region according to an analysis of *woreda*-level data before and after decentralization in both regions. Surveys of beneficiaries reveal that they perceive that service coverage and quality have improved. Beneficiary satisfaction has increased markedly in education, and less conspicuously in water and health services.

In SNNPR, the decentralization to *woredas* in 2002/03 tended to narrow differences in per capita expenditures on education and health across *woredas*. Decentralization disproportionately favored remote (more than 50 kilometers from a zonal capital), food-insecure, and pastoral *woredas,* suggesting that decentralization has been pro-poor. Between 2001 (pre-decentralization) and 2004 (post-decentralization), for example, the aggregate budget for education in SNNPR rose 44 percent in remote *woredas* and just 9 percent in *woredas* located less than 50 kilometers from a zonal capital. A similar trend occurred for health. Aggregate spending on education and health by pastoral *woredas* rose 67–86 percent between 2001 and 2004, while spending by non-pastoral *woredas* rose by just 16–23 percent. Food-insecure *woredas* also gained disproportionately from decentralization, with education budgets rising about 30 percent in food-insecure *woredas* compared to 18 percent in food-secure *woredas.*

Decentralization also narrowed the gap in educational outcomes between disadvantaged and better-off *woredas,* especially in SNNPR. Pastoral, food-insecure, and remote *woredas* gained in terms of the educational outcomes examined (gross enrollment rates, Grade 8 examination pass rates, repetition rates, pupil-teacher ratios, and teacher-section ratios). These results mirror changes in spending patterns, which also disproportionately favored lagging areas in SNNPR.

The changes in education service delivery may also be partly influenced by better deployment of teachers with decentralization. In SNNPR the redeployment of teachers, especially from towns to nearby rural areas, resulted in a more even distribution of teachers across *woredas,* thus partly alleviating problems in schools with very high pupil-teacher ratios. These changes were influenced by the strong sector policy on teacher deployment and placement, and supported by a budget transfer system using the "unit cost" approach adopted by SNNPR.

The decentralization is only one among the myriad of inter-related factors that may have affected service delivery. Sectoral policies in education and health may also have improved service delivery. The policy of using local languages at the lower primary level may have increased school participation, for example. The growing role of communities, parent-teacher associations (PTAs), and other local organizations, which can be measured only qualitatively, may also have contributed to better service delivery. Household surveys have also shown that demand for education has increased over the past decade, as shown by the rising rates of returns for education. Decentralization has also enabled the regions to experiment with innovative service delivery mechanisms such as the use of performance agreements in SNNPR.

. . . But Weaknesses in the System Threaten the Achievement of Human Development Goals

Although social indicators have improved, at the current pace, targets for primary school completion, child and maternal mortality, and clean water and sanitation will not be attained. To increase the pace of improvement, policymakers need to address several weaknesses.

Woredas Need More Funding to Adequately Undertake Service Delivery

A major constraint is the inadequate funding for basic services provided to lower tiers of government. *Woreda* administrations, which are responsible for meeting service provision targets, rely almost exclusively on unconditional block grants from regional governments. About 90 percent of these grants is spent on salaries and operational costs, leaving little for other investments essential to reaching the Millennium Development Goals (MDGs).

The Capacity of Local Governments Needs to Be Increased

Many *woredas* lack skilled personnel. Administrative and technical posts created to handle administrative responsibilities have not been fully filled or have been filled by untrained personnel with limited capacity. Many *woredas* also have poor infrastructure to support transformation, with water, electricity, and communication networks either nonexistent or old and obsolete. Progress is being made on these fronts, as capacity building efforts take hold and upgrading of *woredas* occurs. This progress needs to continue, supported by increases in recurrent and capital budgets for *woredas.* In addition, the role of capacity building programs, such as the Public Sector Capacity Building Project (PSCAP), is key to deepening decentralization.

Need for Clarity in Assignment of Roles Across Tiers of Government

Detailed expenditure assignments by level of government have not been clearly defined. The lack of clarity creates a disconnect between responsibilities and finances at lower tiers of government, severely so at the *woreda* level; leads to duplicated effort and lack of coordination; and deprives each level of government of a point of reference against which to budget in order to meet service delivery objectives. Efforts are being made to address this situation, and regional legal frameworks specifying expenditure assignments are being set up; these efforts need to be supported, and continued progress needs to be made in this area.

Citizens Do Not Hold Service Providers Accountable

Before the start of decentralization, the role of citizens was one of the weakest links in the chain of service delivery in Ethiopia and one of the rationales for decentralization was to strengthen this. Within the decentralized system, the *kebele* council is the forum where citizens could play a role in enforcing accountability of service delivery. But the system is still evolving and initiatives to further strengthen this formal channel of citizens' participation should be welcomed.

Opportunity Costs Prevent Many Households from Using Services

Many poor households in Ethiopia find it difficult to use education and health facilities because the opportunity costs of doing so are very high. Many children are out of school because they work in household enterprises (mostly farms). Not only distance to schools and health facilities, but also distance to water and firewood, reduces their use of education and health services. Even if the other hurdles to improving service delivery are overcome, it may not be possible to reach the MDG targets if the opportunity costs of many households are not reduced.

Policy Recommendations

To accelerate the achievement of human development outcomes, several aspects of decentralization and service delivery need to be improved.

Increase the budget envelop of *woredas* commensurate to their assigned responsibilities for delivering basic services. Lack of adequate resources limits the *woredas'* ability to empower themselves and improve service delivery. Increasing the block grants from the Federal government to the regions and from regions to *woredas* would help redress this situation. In this regard, the commitment by the Federal government to increase total block grant transfers to the regions from 5.5 billion Birr in 2004/05 to 21.56 billion Birr in 2009/10, after reaching 9.4 billion Birr in 2006/07, is very encouraging.

- *Implement an appropriate tax-collection and revenue-sharing mechanism to provide incentives to woredas to diversify and expand their sources of revenue.* To improve *woredas'* resources for service delivery, a revenue-sharing and revenue-assignment mechanism needs to be in place to serve as an incentive for *woredas* to diversify and expand their sources of revenue. Currently, *woredas* collect revenues on behalf of the regions; they are given revenue targets which are not always realistic. If they collect less revenue than the target level, they are often penalized. Conversely, revenues in excess of the targets are often "offset" against the *woredas'* block grant allocations so that *woredas* in effect do not retain any excess revenues, and so have no incentive to collect revenues beyond a certain level. Guidelines on revenue-sharing mechanisms and revenue assignments are needed.
- *Adopt a unit cost or other needs-based approach for determining intergovernmental fiscal transfers.* The data presented in this report indicates that the "unit cost" approach used until recently in SNNPR to allocate block grants to *woredas* did a better job of improving the efficiency of resource allocation across *woredas*. The "unit cost" approach was also much better at addressing service delivery needs than the "three-parameter" approach used in several other regions in Ethiopia. The "three-parameter" approach is also flawed in that it has a built-in bias against large localities. This is especially apparent at the Federal level, where it was used until 2006/07 to determine block grant transfer levels to the regions. Until 2006/07, there was a tight inverse relationship between a region's per-capita transfer and its population—with factors other than the population, such as a region's development level, appearing to have little influence on the final per-capita transfer level.
- *Improve local government capacity by scaling up implementation of the Public Sector Capacity Building Project to increase the use of resources for capacity building at the woreda level.* In this project, utilization of funds is "demand-driven", with regions making applications for funds as needed. The utilization rate has been low, and one of the first priorities should be to increase this rate by boosting the demand for these funds on the part of regions.
- *Improve the capacity and incentives of frontline providers (teachers, health staff, and woreda bureaus).* Human resources are critical for service delivery. The regions need

to create incentive mechanisms to attract and retain qualified staff at the *woreda* level. Regions have been experimenting with incentives such as hardship allowances for teachers and health staff posted in remote or arid lands, and training opportunities for staff in remote areas.

■ *Align sector policies with fiscal decentralization policies to improve impact on service delivery.* The experience of SNNPR has shown that improvements in efficiency in education service delivery could be achieved with better deployment of teachers. This was made possible by two policies working in synergy: (a) the regional education sector policy on deployment and placement of teachers from urban schools with low pupil-teacher ratios to schools with high pupil-teacher ratios and (b) the policy of allocating block grants to *woredas* using the "unit cost" approach which supported the budgets for such teacher reallocation, and which explicitly aims to allocate resources across *woredas* in line with needs.

■ *Clarify the functional roles between regions and woredas.* Legal frameworks and functional assignments between regions and *woredas* should be clearly identified, and *woredas* should be given decisionmaking power over areas for which they have functional responsibility.

■ *Enhance the role of communities.* Community involvement in service delivery has been increasing in Ethiopia. In many regions, communities help out by providing financial contributions and by building schools and health posts. Increasingly, community organizations like the parent-teacher associations (PTAs) are assisting in mobilization and have helped increase enrolment rates in many parts of the country. Regional experiments involving PTAs in the management of schools have been successful in improving service delivery. In this respect it is recommended that such involvement of PTAs in the management of schools be promoted systematically across all regions.

■ *Strengthen transparency and accountability in service delivery.* SNNPR has successfully used performance agreements between the region and *woredas*. The agreements allow for a more transparent monitoring of inputs and outputs in service delivery between regions and *woredas*, providing a mechanism for ensuring accountability and effective resource management. Such agreements should be adopted throughout the country. More formally, one should ensure that citizen voice can be strengthened within the purview of the *Kebele* Council. Furthermore, citizens can be involved in local management of services through PTAs and local health boards. PTAs can coordinate the use of community scorecards of school performance while participatory planning and monitoring by citizens can be used to strengthen the accountability of *woreda* and *kebele* councils. Citizen report cards, communicating the importance of service quality and coverage, can be an input into a system of evaluation of local governments against agreed performance contracts. In addition, ongoing initiatives to post *woreda* and regional budgets in public places, and to present budgets in formats that are readily understood by citizens, should be strengthened and encouraged. It is essential to promote the sharing of experiences from all these experiments across all regions.

■ *Use public information campaigns to improve education and health outcomes.* Child health outcomes could be improved significantly by providing nutrition information to mothers or helping households understand the value of boiling water, use of oral rehydration salts, and hand washing. Decentralization and citizen empowerment should magnify the effects of public information campaigns. *Woredas* and municipalities could use health extension workers and community or municipal radios to disseminate knowledge on child health.

- *Systematically evaluate key reforms.* Ethiopia is in the process of implementing a major transformation of its political economy. Far-reaching reforms have been adopted in school curricula, the structure of the education system, school fees, the structure of the health system, user fees, and modes of delivery of primary health services through health extension workers. However, no systematic attempt has been made to evaluate many of these interventions to understand what works well and what does not. Rigorous evaluation of these reforms is needed to ensure that the proposed scaling up is informed by lessons learned to date from local as well as international experience.

CHAPTER 1

Improvements in Health and Education Services

This report seeks to identify changes in human development outcomes in a period of deepening decentralization and to suggest how the country's decentralized governance structure could be improved to increase access to, as well as the quality of, relevant services.

A key message of the report is that the decentralized governance structure helped facilitate improvements in service delivery and human development outcomes but that weaknesses in that structure can derail these gains. The report argues that while policymakers, providers, and citizens must work together to strengthen accountability mechanisms, there is a particular need to strengthen local government and enhance the role of service beneficiaries.

The report focuses on key actors and their roles in accelerating progress toward achieving the MDGs in Ethiopia. It complements rather than duplicates other recent studies. The education and health country status reports for Ethiopia (World Bank 2005a, 2005b) are rich in both content and policy recommendations. They examine in greater detail the determinants of education and health outcomes and propose many insightful policy options, using both administrative and household survey data. The Poverty Assessment (World Bank 2005c) draws on and enriches the findings in the country status reports by linking these outcomes to poverty. It extends the analysis to cover more general questions of economic opportunities and welfare. This study also draws on the Pilot Citizens Report Card prepared by the Poverty Action Network of Ethiopia (PANE 2005), the *Woreda*-City Government Benchmarking Survey conducted by GTZ-Selam Development Consultants (2005), an intergovernmental fiscal review by Heymans and Mussa (2004), a Fiduciary Assessment report (Government of Ethiopia 2005b), and an Oxfam study on implementation of decentralization policy in Ethiopia (Adal 2005).

The report is organized as follows. This chapter reports on trends in human development indicators and government social expenditures in Ethiopia over the past 15 years. Chapter 2 describes the phasing in of Ethiopia's decentralization plan and presents a framework of mechanisms of accountability for providing services. Chapter 3 examines the scope of decentralization in Ethiopia and the use of intergovernmental transfers. Chapter 4 presents some of the data collected for this report on changes in budget allocation behavior at the *woreda* level before and after decentralization and the effects on allocations for the social sectors. It also examines changes in key service delivery outcomes at the *woreda* level. Chapter 5 examines some of the constraints to improved service delivery and proposes ways of increasing resources at decentralized levels, of improving the capacity of local governments and service providers, and of involving citizens in service delivery in a more robust and effective way. It stresses the critical need to clarify functional expenditure assignments and rules governing the allocation of block grants, to establish guidelines for communities' role in service delivery, and to empower communities by providing them with more information.

Changes in Outcomes over the Past 15 Years

During the past 15 years, Ethiopia has witnessed rapid improvements in health and education outcomes. Enrollment rates at all levels have risen substantially, albeit from a low base (Figure 1.1). The total number of primary schools has risen steadily over the last 40 years, with a recent sharp acceleration starting in 2004. School enrollment surged from 1993 onwards.

Coverage in health services also increased, although to a smaller extent than in education. For most Ethiopians, health facilities are closer than they were 10 years ago, and their rate of usage is higher, with the annual number of per capita visits to health facilities increasing from 0.3 in 1993 to 0.4 in 2005. Progress was also made in child health outcomes. Immunization rates for DPT 3 remain low, but they reached 60 percent by 2005, up from 46 percent in 1995. 80 percent of the population is now immunized against polio.

Coverage of water services increased, with the proportion of households with access to safe drinking water (water from a tap or covered well) rising from 19.1 percent in 1996 to 35.9 percent in 2004 (GOE/MoFED 2005a). Over the same period, the proportion of households with access to improved sanitation (flush toilet or pit latrine) rose from 13.0 percent to 30.6 percent.

Was Decentralization Responsible?

Basic coverage accelerated during the period of decentralization, but without further analysis it is not possible to conclude that decentralization was responsible for the change, as decentralization was part of a package of government policies and actions that included school construction, teacher hiring, provision for local language instruction at the primary level, and adjustment of the school calendar (especially in rural areas) to accommodate the agricultural cycle of farm households.

Government spending on education and health rose, both as a share of GDP and as a share of total government spending (Table 1.1). Public education expenditures almost tripled between 1999/2000 and 2005/2006 in real terms, rising from 3.1 percent to 5.9 per-

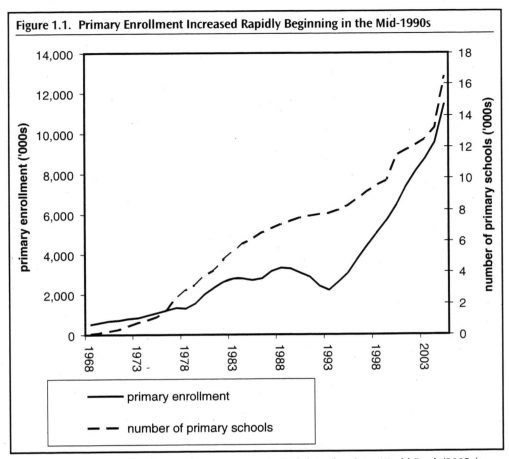

Figure 1.1. Primary Enrollment Increased Rapidly Beginning in the Mid-1990s

Source: World Bank staff estimates from survey and administrative data; World Bank (2005a);
data from the Annual Abstracts on education.

cent of GDP over this period. Over the same period, real public health expenditures almost doubled, rising from 1.1 percent to 2.0 percent of GDP.

The share of government spending going to education almost doubled between the collapse of the Derg government in 1990 and the beginning of decentralization to the regions in 1993/94 (Figure 1.2). Given the relationship between spending on education and primary school enrollment, it is tempting to conclude that most of the growth in primary enrollment was driven by increases in public spending on education. Such a conclusion would be misguided, however, for two reasons.

First, some of the growth in spending was on secondary and tertiary education, where spending has risen more rapidly than with primary education. Second, a closer look at the relationship between spending and primary enrollment indicates that observed increases in government spending are insufficient to account for the rapid rise in enrollment, which rose much more rapidly than government spending (Figure 1.2). In short, there is a momentum to enrollment growth that cannot be explained by the increase in public spending alone.

Table 1.1. Index of Real Government Expenditures and Spending as Percentage of GDP, 1999–2005

Item	1999/2000 Actual	2000/01 Pre-Actual	2001/02 Pre-Actual	2002/03 Pre-Actual	2003/04 Pre-Actual	2004/05 Pre-Actual	2005/06 Pre-Actual
Index of Real Expenditures (1999/2000 = 100)							
Total government expenditure	100	97.8	103.0	114.1	107.1	121.7	129.2
Defense	100	51.0	43.4	33.8	32.6	36.3	33.4
Debt servicing	100	101.5	101.8	107.3	87.5	76.7	71.2
Agriculture and natural resources	100	156.7	148.7	173.3	223.5	342.3	368.0
Roads	100	216.6	203.3	225.7	201.0	264.6	369.5
Education	100	138.6	168.8	197.6	230.8	252.2	294.2
Health	100	236.9	220.7	187.2	149.2	191.1	190.1
Other sectors	100	96.5	121.6	156.1	122.0	116.0	107.9
Percentage of GDP							
Total government expenditure	26.7	23.0	21.6	29.1	27.2	29.3	33.4
Defense	10.6	4.8	3.6	3.4	3.3	3.5	3.4
Debt servicing	1.7	1.6	1.4	1.8	1.5	1.2	1.2
Agriculture and natural resources	2.0	2.7	2.3	3.3	4.2	6.2	7.1
Roads	1.4	2.6	2.2	3.0	2.6	3.3	5.0
Education	2.6	3.1	3.4	4.8	5.6	5.8	7.3
Health	0.8	1.7	1.4	1.5	1.2	1.4	1.5
Other sectors	7.6	6.4	7.2	11.3	8.8	7.9	7.9

Source: Data provided by MoFED.

One source of this additional momentum is the change in policies, especially the teaching of primary school in local languages and the adoption of a flexible calendar in rural areas that takes into consideration the agricultural cycle. Another source may have been the shift in demand for education and health that is likely to have taken place among the households and individuals most likely to invest in health and education. The rate of return to education in Ethiopia was about 6 percent in the early 1990s (Suleiman 1995; Weir and Knight 1996; Krishnan 1996). More recent studies on the demand for education, based on surveys conducted in early 2001, show that returns had risen to 8–12 percent (World Bank 2005a). The end of civil strife, the return of law and order, and the establishment of a government of national unity may have convinced many households and individuals that the new social order was irreversible in the medium to long term. These perceptions may have

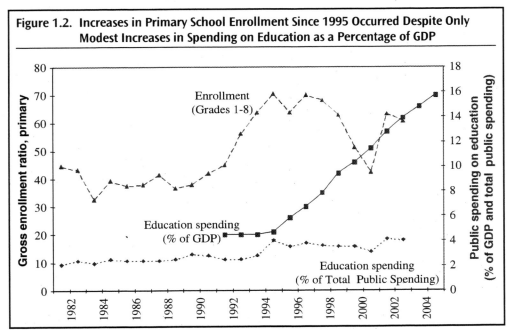

Figure 1.2. Increases in Primary School Enrollment Since 1995 Occurred Despite Only Modest Increases in Spending on Education as a Percentage of GDP

Source: World Bank (2005a).

encouraged many households to make long-term investments in their own education and health and that of their children. This shift in demand is unlikely to have been a major cause of the increase in enrollment, however, because the opportunity costs of education remain formidable, as discussed in Chapter 5.

Consultations with a wide array of Ethiopians—from *woreda* officials to community residents—reveal several advantages of decentralization. According to the people interviewed for this study, locally relevant solutions to problems are now found promptly through more democratic and representative processes. Plans are locally drafted and approved, budgets are managed locally, and control is more effective. Budget shortfalls are dealt with more fairly under decentralization, and the relationship between tiers of government is character-ized more by partnerships than the more remote and bureaucratic structures that prevailed before decentralization (Halvorsen, Smith, and Shenkut 2005).

Beneficiary satisfaction is improving. Three consumer satisfaction assessments—the Welfare Monitoring Survey 2004, the Citizens' Report Card (PANE 2005), and the Ethiopia Participatory Poverty Assessment 2004/05 (GOE/MoFED 2005b)—point to moderately improving service provision in health, education, and water services. Similar findings were obtained in the *Woreda*-City Government Benchmarking Survey (GTZ-Selam Development Consultants 2005).

The Citizens' Report Card provides feedback from users of public services on access to, quality of, and adequacy of services. It is based on a sample of 3,829 households in 10 *woreda*s and municipalities in Afar, Dire Dawa, Oromiya, Tigray, and the Southern Nations, Nationalities and Peoples Region (SNNPR). A surprising result from this survey is the moderate level of satisfaction with health services, given the relatively poor coverage

Table 1.2. User Satisfaction with Government Health Services, 2005

Measure	Dire Dawa	Oromiya	SNNPR	Tigray
Time taken to attend	63	54	57	79
Behavior of staff/doctor	60	56	58	80
Overall satisfaction	46	50	46	54

Note: Figures reflect percentage of respondents that are completely satisfied.
Source: PANE (2005).

Table 1.3. User Satisfaction with School Services, 2005

Measure	Dire Dawa	Oromiya	SNNPR	Tigray
Quality of teaching	76	68	75	87
School building	80	51	58	68
Toilet	69	58	75	49
Behavior of teachers	73	71	78	90
Overall satisfaction	72	59	56	41

Note: Figures reflect percentage of respondents that are completely satisfied.
Source: PANE (2005).

and quality of care of the facilities (Table 1.2). About half of respondents reported being satisfied with the services received at health facilities. Satisfaction was highest in Tigray, where 80 percent of clients reported being satisfied with the behavior of doctors.

Satisfaction with the quality and behavior of teachers is also surprisingly high among users, across the country, possibly as a result of improvement in the qualifications of lower primary level teachers, 96 percent of whom now have Teachers Training Institutes certificates and a rising proportion of whom have College of Teachers Education diplomas (Table 1.3). Almost two-thirds of respondents were satisfied with school infrastructure, one of the key areas of improvement in service delivery at the *woreda* level. For most households, schools are within 5 kilometers from home. In some *woreda*s in Tigray, however, about a third of children travel more than 5 kilometers to school. While textbooks and teaching aids are usually available in schools, toilet and water facilities are severely lacking, with just 10 percent of schools in Tigray, 25 percent in SNNPR, and 33 percent in Oromiya having toilets.

CHAPTER 2

Decentralization and the Delivery of Basic Services

Ethiopia has made considerable progress toward meeting the Millennium Development Goals (MDGs) (Table 2.1). In 2005 nearly 75 percent of Ethiopian children were enrolled in primary schools, the result of an impressive 9 percent annual growth in enrollment since 1993. Similar expansion was achieved at the secondary and post-secondary levels. Immunization coverage for measles stood at 57 percent, up from 40 percent in 1995. Stunting fell from 66 percent in 1996 to 47 percent in 2005, while under-five mortality declined from 21 percent in 1990 to 14 percent in 2003. The percentage of Ethiopians with access to clean water rose from 19 percent in 1995 to 36 percent in 2005.

Phasing in Decentralization

Improvements in health and education outcomes in the past 15 years occurred at a time of massive decentralization in Ethiopia. Ethiopia introduced decentralization as the strategic tool for empowering citizens and devolving power to lower levels, following the Constitution. This, in turn, was expected to establish a conducive environment for enhancing the delivery of basic services.

The decentralization process was implemented in two phases. The first phase created a four-tier governance structure, consisting of the center, the regions (nine ethnic-based states plus the cities of Addis Ababa and Dire Dawa), the zones, and the *woredas*.[1] During this phase, the regional governments were given responsibility for delivering all education (except tertiary and secondary teacher training) and health services. To facilitate these

---

1. Ethiopia has 700 *woredas,* with an average population of just over 110,000.

Table 2.1. Trends in Service Delivery, 1995/96–2004/05 (percent)

Indicator	Year				Percentage Change 1996–2004	Percentage Change 2000–2004
	1995/96	1997/98	1999/00	2004/05		
Primary (Grades 1–8)						
Gross enrollment rate	37	52	61	74	37	13
Literacy rate	26	27	29	38	12	9
Under-five child immunization						
Measles	39	47	48	57	18	9
BCG	35	47	46	55	20	9
Access to safe drinking water	19	24	28	36	17	8

Source: PASDEP (Government of Ethiopia/MoFED, 2005a).

functions, thousands of civil servants were redeployed from the center to the regions. The zones and the *woredas* are lower-level tiers of the regional governments, with *woredas* below the level of zones.

During the second half of the 1990s, the Government, together with development partners, conducted a number of studies to identify the factors that hindered public sector efficiency, grassroots empowerment, and accountability. An important lesson learned from these studies was that *woredas* had very limited fiscal or administrative autonomy with which to respond to the needs of their constituencies.

In response to this finding, in 2002/03 the Government initiated the second phase of decentralization with a series of legal, fiscal, and administrative reforms beginning with four of the largest regions (Amhara, Oromiya, SNNPR, and Tigray), which together account for 87 percent of Ethiopia's population. Under this phase, some control was also devolved to the *woreda* level, and eventually urban administrations with *woreda* status and responsibilities were created in urban areas. (Important note: Throughout this document, the term "*woreda*" includes urban administrations by definition, unless otherwise stated.) Within the four regions, *woredas* now manage about 45 percent of regional public expenditures. This phase of decentralization seeks to empower communities to engage in development interventions, improve local democratic governance, and enhance the scope and quality of the delivery of basic services at the local level.

The new governance framework establishes the foundations for consolidating accountability mechanisms for better services. It delegates responsibility for service delivery to local governments (Figure 2.1). Clarification of these responsibilities continues to be worked out across tiers of government. The new framework also devolves substantial control over real resources (personnel, assets, and finances, through block grants) to subnational governments (regions and *woredas*). It provides a platform for citizen participation in politics and the enforcement of agreements. The opening of service delivery to private and nongovernmental actors and the empowering of civil society, though just beginning, are promising steps.

While decentralization has empowered local decision makers to set priorities in line with local demand, fiscal and human resources remain a major impediment. *Woredas* have had to manage carefully to meet basic recurrent requirements, mainly salaries, leaving few resources for capital investment, a much needed requirement for expanding services. These constraints are analyzed in Chapter 5.

While human development outcomes have improved, far too many children remain out of school, are in poor health, and die from easily preventable diseases. In education, arguably the most successful effort, at least 4 million children are not served by any school, and many children who have access to a school cannot attend or are not learning, for a variety of reasons. Ethiopia's indicators still lag behind those observed in other poor countries, and progress in many areas—service quality, equity of access, complementary services—has not been as rapid or has deteriorated. In both education and health, the quality of inputs (staff, books, drugs) is inadequate; in water, sanitation, and electricity, huge inequities of access between rich and poor remain.

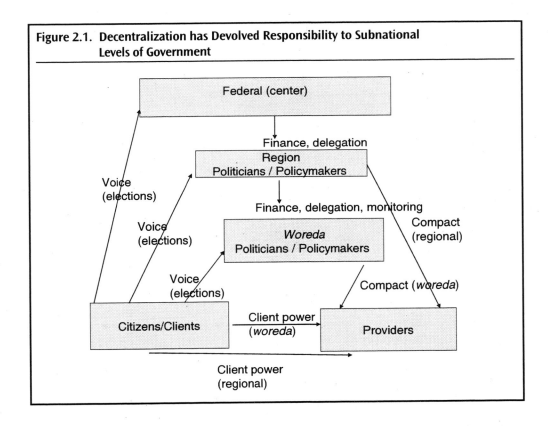

Figure 2.1. Decentralization has Devolved Responsibility to Subnational Levels of Government

A Framework for Understanding Service Delivery Outcomes

In the past, analysis of outcomes focused on the interactions between individual and household variables (preferences, effort, prices, income) and the availability, quality, and financing arrangements within sectors. This focus promoted technical fixes and larger budgets, both of which, while important, were found insufficient.

To broaden the focus of the analysis, the *World Development Report 2004: Making Services Work for Poor People* called for a more encompassing approach. The key message of that report is that improving outcomes requires making services work for all people, especially the poor. Doing so calls for understanding, establishing, and strengthening a service delivery framework, or chain.

The framework adopted in the *World Development Report 2004* focuses on the behavior of actors within the chain, who are linked by accountability mechanisms (Figure 2.2). The chain is defined by the roles of four actors: politicians/policymakers; organizational providers (public, private, nongovernmental organizations); frontline professionals (doctors, nurses, teachers, and so forth); and citizens/clients (patients, students, parents, voters). The accountability relationships are defined by rules and arrangements that include delegation, financing, performance, information, and enforcement.

Figure 2.2.   Accountability for Providing Services Can Follow a Long Route or a Short Route

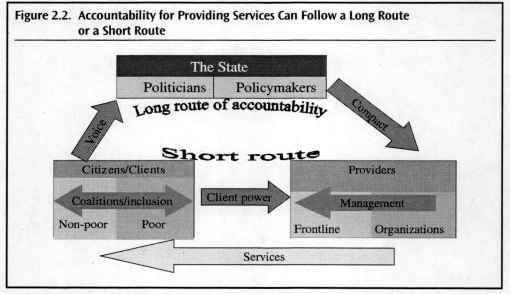

Source: World Development Report 2004.

The framework identifies a long route and a short route of influence. Along the long route, citizens use political institutions to hold politicians and policymakers accountable, and politicians and policymakers enter into agreements with providers to deliver services to citizens. Citizens delegate policymaking and the allocation of resources across competing needs to politicians and policymakers, who use providers to implement these policies. Politicians and policymakers provide providers with policy priorities and resources, with which providers manage the frontline professionals who run services.

Along the short route, the influence of citizens/clients on providers is more direct. Citizens/clients can switch providers, they can participate in decisionmaking, and they can use better information to monitor the actions of providers and enforce compliance.

All of these relationships are important; any weak link in the chain can lead to service delivery failure. In an ideal world, the benefits from services will be maximized if both the long and the short routes function: politicians/policymakers respond to citizen/client demands by establishing strong agreements, which citizens/clients (together with politicians/policymakers) monitor and enforce by exercising power over providers. How well these accountability mechanisms, especially the power of citizens/clients over politicians/policymakers and providers, work often depends on a country's political economy.

The framework depicted in Figure 2.2 suggests that along the long route, accountability is best accomplished in an environment in which citizens/clients are principals—that is, actors who delegate policymaking to politicians/policymakers but wield the power to remove politicians from office for poor performance. To retain the support of citizens/clients in every electoral cycle, politicians/policymakers establish and enforce strong agreements with providers. The long route thus has a better chance of working in a well-functioning democratic environment.

For most of its history, Ethiopia has not had a competitive democratic system. Under both the monarchy and communist rule, citizens had no voice in Ethiopia. Since 1991 Ethiopia has had a constitutional democracy. Three national elections have been held, the second in the midst of a war. The third, held in May 2005, appeared to usher in more reforms, although post-election violence has slowed the otherwise orderly democratic process.

Ethiopia's electoral system is still new, and it has not always been viewed as completely free or competitive. But there is now space for new and hitherto excluded groups to organize and to voice their demands for better representation and access to services. Whether the full potential of the emerging long route of accountability will be maximized remains to be seen.

More far-reaching has been the administrative and fiscal dimensions of the decentralization process. The motivation for Ethiopia's decentralization effort was—in line with the Constitution—to improve on the record of centralized control and allocation of resources, which ignored local preferences and neglected entire regions. Decentralization appears to be an attempt to implement and reap the benefits of the accountability framework by reducing the distance between citizens and politicians/policymakers.

CHAPTER 3

The Scope of Decentralization and Intergovernmental Fiscal Transfers

Regional constitutions and urban proclamations have defined the broad functional assignments of local governments since decentralization. Regional governments are still fine-tuning the detailed assignments of both expenditures and revenues. This chapter describes the kinds of services and functions assigned to lower tiers of government. It examines the relationships between *woreda*-level governments (*woreda* administrations) and governments at the zonal, region, and federal levels. It also describes the financing of these services, reviewing trends in intergovernmental fiscal transfers from the federal government to the regions and from the regions to the *woreda*s (including urban administrations by definition).

Subnational Structures

Decentralization in Ethiopia established nine regions (Afar, Amhara, Benishangul-Gumuz, Gambella, Harari, Oromiya, SNNPR, Somali, and Tigray) and two city administrations (Addis Ababa and Dire Dawa). The regions are divided into zones, *woreda*s/urban administrations, and kebeles (village areas, with an average population of 5,000). The city administrations of Addis Ababa and Dire Dawa have different structures but are considered the equivalent of regions.

Over the past two years, the zones in most regions have become arms of the regional government. The *woreda*s are considered the key local government units in each region, with significant responsibility for providing basic services.

The local government landscape follows similar patterns across regions. There are 140 local governments (128 rural *woreda*s and 12 urban administrations) in Amhara, 284 local governments (248 rural *woreda*s and 36 urban administrations) in Oromiya, 156 local governments (137 rural *woreda*s and 19 urban administrations) in SNNPR, and 47 local governments (34 rural *woreda*s and 13 urban administrations) in Tigray. However, these numbers are constantly changing; the number of *woreda*s has been steadily increasing over the last few years because of frequent splitting of existing *woreda*s to create new ones.

Regional Governments

Each region has at its apex a regional council, with regional council members representing each *woreda* directly elected. Councils have legislative and executive authority to direct the internal affairs of the levels of government under their jurisdiction. Administrative functions are executed by regional bureaus, structured on a sector basis. In each region, a cabinet, under a regional president, performs the executive role. The regions are governed by city proclamations and other local government legislation, but all are also in the process of updating this to deal with complex demands of the decentralization structure. The role of regions and zones in relation to local governments varies from region to region.

Woreda Administrations

The tripartite structure of council, executive committee, and sector bureaus is replicated at the *woreda* level. *Woreda* councils consist of directly elected representatives from each kebele in the *woreda*. The *woreda* councils have dual accountability, upward to the regional cabinet/council and downward to the electorate. *Woreda* cabinets consist of about a dozen members, drawn from elected representatives and heads of sectoral offices. The main constitutional powers and duties of the *woreda* council and its executive are preparing and approving the annual *woreda* development plans and budgets and monitoring their implementation; setting certain tax rates and collecting local taxes and levies (principally land use taxes, agricultural income taxes, sales taxes, and user fees); remitting a portion of the local tax take to the zone; administering the fiscal resources available to the *woreda* (from own sources and transfers); constructing and maintaining low-grade rural tracks, water points, and *woreda*-level administrative infrastructure (offices, houses); administering primary schools and health institutions; managing agricultural development activities; and protecting natural resources.

Urban Administrations

Urban administrations—often also called urban local government administrations or simply urban governments—have the same status as *woredas*. They perform state and municipal functions. State functions include health, education, and agricultural services. Municipal functions include preparation, approval, and implementation of development plans; assessment and collection of allowable municipal revenues; provision of internal roads and bridges; provision of markets, slaughter houses, terminals, public gardens, recreational areas, and other public facilities; regulation of cleanliness and provision of solid waste, water, sewerage, and drainage services; management of urban land and provision of urban land services; and delivery of miscellaneous services, including fire protection, libraries, public toilets, street lighting, nursery schools, and ambulance services.

In addition to its 84 urban administrations, Ethiopia has 863 municipalities/towns. These municipalities are under the jurisdiction of the *woredas* and generally carry out municipal functions. They do not have *woreda* status and do not carry out state functions. They typically do not receive transfers from the regional or other governments, relying on own sources of revenue. It is expected that an increasing number of municipalities will seek to become urban administrations with *woreda* status in the future.

Kebele Administrations

The kebeles do not enjoy the same constitutional formality as regions. Their administrations consist of an elected council (in principle of 100 members), an executive committee of five to seven citizens, and a social court. The main responsibilities of the kebele council and executive committee are preparing an annual development plan, ensuring the collection of land and agricultural income tax, organizing local labor and in-kind contributions to development activities, and resolving conflicts within the community through the social courts.

Decentralization of Functions and Responsibilities

Decentralization devolved expenditure and revenue responsibilities for education, health, and water and sanitation to different tiers of government (Table 3.1). The definition of functions is evolving, although across regions the trend is toward decentralizing basic service delivery functions to the *woredas* and assigning higher order functions—such as provision of hospital care—to regional governments. Tertiary services, such as tertiary education, standard setting, and operation of specialized hospitals, remain the responsibility of the federal government.

Allocation of Responsibilities for Education

Woredas are responsible for establishing and administering basic education services, including primary schools (Grades 1–8), the first cycle of secondary school (Grades 9–10), and adult education. Their responsibilities include supervising these schools; printing and distributing primary school textbooks; and establishing and administering primary boarding schools.

In the delivery of basic services, the *woredas* are tasked with planning and developing short- and long-term plans for education in their jurisdictions and ensuring that plans are implemented, by both government and nongovernmental schools, according to the standards set at the regional and federal levels. This function includes planning the location of new schools in kebeles ensuring equity in access to education; strengthening educational supervision; enhancing community participation by supporting citizen participation in educational administration; and encouraging and supporting parent-teacher associations (PTAs).

In principle, the *woreda*s are responsible for hiring elementary school teachers, deploying them to specific schools, and paying their salaries. In collaboration with the *Woreda* Education and Training Board, they make and implement decisions about disciplinary measures regarding school heads. In SNNPR the zones and special *woredas* are responsible for translating the curriculum into local languages and providing technical support and supervision to the *woreda* bureaus. Most zones are made up of several *woredas;* special *woredas* are different in that they are single *woredas* that also have the status of a zone.

Table 3.1. Assignment of Expenditure and Revenue Responsibilities for Education, Health, and Water and Sanitation, by Tier of Government, circa 2005

Tier of government	Expenditure and functional responsibilities	Revenue sources
Federal	National standard setting for education, health, and water and sanitation Tertiary education Specialized/referral hospitals	Custom duties; export and import taxes or levies; income and enterprise taxes; taxes on proceeds of national lottery, stamp duties, income from federal monopolies, and fees from transport services (road, air, water, and rail).[1]
Regional	Standard setting for primary and secondary education and regional health Vocational and technical training, teacher training institutes, and medium-level colleges Hospitals and referral hospitals Control and prevention of HIV/AIDS Immunization Coordination and execution of civil service reform programs at regional level Policy setting on regional water resource development and protection Second cycle of secondary education (Grades 11–12)	Grants from federal government (70–80 percent of revenues) Income taxes (personal, sales, corporate, profit, property, and other) Fees on agricultural land, licensing, royalty, forest resources, water use, and other activities Fees on health services, such as drugs
Woreda	Coordination of school management and cost-sharing activities Coordination of primary preventive and curative health care activities Establishment and administration of primary schools (Grades 1–8) and fist cycle of secondary education (Grades 9–10) Implementation of health extension Construction and administration of health stations and health posts and administration of clinics Control and prevention of HIV/AIDS and malaria Immunization Coordination and management of drinking water supplies	Grants from regional government (80–90 percent of revenues)[2] Personal income tax, agricultural income tax, rural land use tax, rental income tax, licenses and fees

Notes:
1. The federal government shares revenues from profit, excise, and personal income taxes; dividend taxes; and income derived from mining, petroleum, and gas operations with the regions. Currently there are no export taxes, but the Federal government has the mandate to impose them.
2. Many municipalities do not receive block grants but are self-financing.
Source: Government of Ethiopia (2005a); Amhara National Regional State (2005).

The zones and regions are responsible for establishing and administering the second cycle of secondary education (Grades 11–12), technical and vocational schools, special schools, teacher training institutes, and medium-level colleges. Regions are also responsible for printing and distributing books for secondary schools; administering boarding schools in pastoral areas; formulating regional education policy and strategy; preparing curriculum for primary schools; administering educational radio broadcast centers; providing technical and material support; training primary school teachers, and ensuring that national education sector service standards are met.

In large regions like Oromiya and SNNPR, the zones have much more responsibilities than in other regions and are performing functions assigned to regions. In regions with large zones, the zones coordinate the distribution of textbooks and other educational materials, and provide support to *woredas*. In many regions, zones are assigned functions that cannot be implemented by *woredas* because of capacity constraints. These constraints, arising from the lack of clarity in responsibilities and expenditure assignments, are described more fully in Chapter 5.

Regional governments also coordinate the efforts of other levels of government, NGOs, and other public organizations toward meeting educational objectives in the region. They work with the zones as well as the *woredas* in deploying teachers, especially graduates of regional institutions, to *woredas*.

The federal government is responsible for establishing and administering tertiary institutions; developing national education policy; establishing national education standards and monitoring observance by regions; supporting regional curriculum development efforts for primary education, secondary education, and technical and vocational education; providing technical and professional support to regional education bureaus; setting standards for national examinations and standards of certificates; establishing professional standards for teachers; and supporting the training provided by the regions. In cooperation with relevant bodies, the federal government has devised mechanisms to enhance educational support to girls, women, and those from minority groups.

Allocation of Responsibilities for Health

The *woredas* are responsible for coordinating primary preventive and curative health care and implementing health extension; constructing and administering health stations and health posts; administering clinics; and preventing and controlling HIV/AIDS and malaria. Their responsibilities include the hiring of health staff assigned to health stations, health posts, and clinics.

The regions are responsible for formulating regional health policy; coordinating health extension activities; establishing and administering training institutions and junior colleges for junior health professionals; training health professionals; providing technical support to zones and *woredas*; establishing and administering health examination centers; building and maintaining referral hospitals; coordinating the control of communicable diseases; purchasing and distributing medical equipment and medicines; and preventing and controlling HIV/AIDS. In large regions the zones are responsible for providing technical support to *woredas;* establishing and administering zonal and district hospitals; constructing and administering pharmacies; and preventing and controlling HIV/AIDS.

The federal government is responsible for establishing and administering specialized and referral hospitals. It is also responsible for setting national health policy; establishing national health standards and basic criteria for health; and monitoring implementation across regions.

Allocation of Responsibilities for Water Services

The *woredas* are tasked with providing support to communities to administer water schemes; develop springs; build hand-dug wells; handle minor and moderate maintenance of water schemes; and promote indigenous irrigation schemes.

The zones are responsible for providing the *woredas* with training and technical support; constructing water supply projects in small towns; and designing, building, and maintaining medium-size springs and wells.

The regions are responsible for formulating water development and conservation strategy; providing training on operation and maintenance of watering schemes; evaluating the need for, designing, building, and maintaining boreholes; setting standards for different watering scheme services; evaluating the need for and building town water supply facilities; and evaluating the need for, designing, and building large- and medium-scale irrigation projects.

The federal government is responsible for setting national standards for water and sanitation, including the use of water, lakes, and rivers linking and crossing Ethiopia's national boundaries.

Financing Social Services Through Intergovernmental Transfers

Public financing of basic social services is implemented through intergovernmental fiscal transfers from the federal government to the regions as well as from regional governments to *woredas*. In implementing the decentralization strategy, the Government has developed a body of rules that govern transfers from one tier to the next. The most important source of financing of the regional and *woreda*-level governments is the block grant transfer from the next higher level of government. This section describes the features of the allocation rules and recent trends in their implementation.

Fiscal Transfers from Federal Governments to the Regions

A major transfer of federal resources to the regions takes place through the federal grant system, which consists of block grants and specific-purpose grants. Most of the transfer takes place as block grants. In 2003/04, the Federal government tried to introduce a particular type of formula (described below) to make allocations of block grants to each region. However, the formula—when applied to the entire pool of resources available for block grants—was found to provide inadequate allocations to some regions, especially the ones with increasing recurrent costs and expanding numbers of public facilities. Therefore, it was decided that in every year from 2003/04 onwards, a two-step allocation process would be used. First, each region would obtain the same recurrent allocation as in 2002/03; this would be a minimum allocation. Second, after making these initial minimum allocations, the formula would be used to distribute additional resources across regions.

From 2003/04 to 2006/07, the above two-step allocation process was used to make Federal block grant allocations across regions. The formula used for the second step of this allocation process is called the "three-parameter" block grant allocation formula. It takes into consideration the population size (65 percent), poverty and development level (25 percent), and an index of revenue effort and sectoral performance (10 percent) of each region. One problem is that the underlying data (on poverty and development level, etc.) used to apply the formula were not updated since 2003/04, even though the formula was used to make allocations every year from 2003/04 to 2006/07. The method for applying this formula is given in Appendix A. Note that some adjustments were made to the formula described to account for recurring budget deficits.

The aim of the federal block grant transfer is to address the vertical imbalances in revenue versus expenditure assignments between the federal and regional administrations.

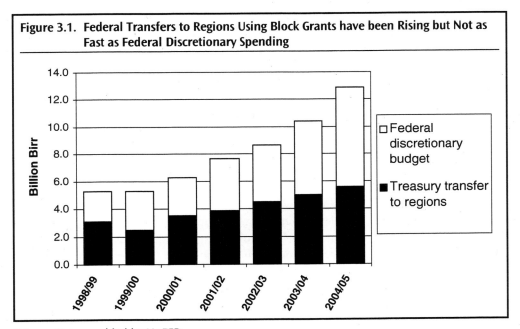

Figure 3.1. **Federal Transfers to Regions Using Block Grants have been Rising but Not as Fast as Federal Discretionary Spending**

Source: Data provided by MoFED.

The trends in absolute amounts of federal block grant transfers to regions can be seen in Figure 3.1 for the period from 1998/99 to 2004/05. It shows that these transfers are increasing, although not rising as fast as the federal discretionary budget. On the other hand, the faster growth in the federal discretionary budget can be attributed to a large increase in funding for Special Purpose Grants, which are included under the federal discretionary spending category even though they are executed at the regional level. On a per capita basis, the block grant allocations to regions in 2005/06 are given in Table 3.2 below. The data show a wide variation in per capita transfers to regions ranging from close to Birr 95 in Amhara, Oromiya and SNNPR; to Birr 603 in Gambella.

Table 3.2. A Wide Variation in Per Capita Block Grant Transfers to Regions

	Population (millions) 2005/06	Per-Capita Block Grant Transfer from Treasury Sources 2005/06 (A)	Per-Capita Block Grant Transfer from Treasury and External Sources 2005/06 (B)	Regional Own Revenue Per Capita 2005/06 (C)	Per-Capita Budget from Own Revenues and Treasury-Source Block Grant Transfers (A+C) 2005/06
Tigray	4.28	117	127	70	187
Afar	1.37	214	226	29	243
Amhara	18.87	81	93	20	101
Oromyia	26.18	89	95	24	113
Somali	4.27	111	117	14	125
Benshangul-G	0.62	335	353	55	390
SNNP	14.70	93	98	18	111
Gambella	0.24	590	603	45	636
Harari	0.19	510	530	111	621
Diredawa	0.39	306	316	84	390

Note: Addis Ababa is excluded from the above table, since it is mostly self-sufficient and does not receive any block grant transfer from Treasury sources. All figures other than in the "Population" column are in Birr.
Source: Data provided by MoFED.

The three regions receiving the lowest per capita transfers in 2005/06 were also the largest regions in terms of population: Oromiya, Amhara, and SNNPR. This illustrates the built-in "bias" that the "three-parameter" formula has against larger regions, if one looks at per capita allocations. Because of the design of the formula, there is a very tight inverse relationship between a region's population and its per capita transfer (Figure 3.2). The relationship is so tight that factors other than population, such as the development level of a region, appear to have little influence on the final level of per capita transfer of a region. The reasons for this, and some of the problems associated with the formula, are discussed in Appendix A.

To illustrate the main point of the previous paragraph, Figure 3.2 depicts the fact that the very small region of Harari received a much higher per-capita block grant transfer in 2005/06 than the much larger region of SNNPR. Yet Harari—a predominantly urban region—is generally considered to be much richer and more developed than SNNPR. According to the 1999/2000 Household Income, Consumption and Expenditure Survey (HICES), for example, the proportion of people living in absolute poverty and in moderate poverty were much lower in Harari (26 and 42 percent respectively) than in SNNPR (51 and 69 percent).

The "three-parameter" formula has a number of problems besides a bias against large and poor regions. In particular, the formula does not take into account the greater needs that some regions may have over others, after controlling for differences in population and development level.

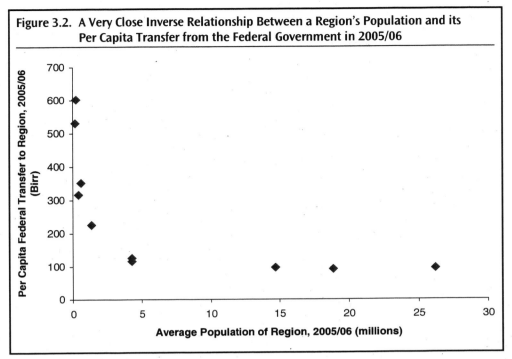

Figure 3.2. A Very Close Inverse Relationship Between a Region's Population and its Per Capita Transfer from the Federal Government in 2005/06

Source: Data provided by MoFED.

For the abovementioned reasons, starting from 2007/08, the Federal government is gradually switching over to a new formula based on a "fiscal equalization" approach. Among other things, this new approach is "needs-based" in the sense that recurrent funding—which accounts for the bulk of total funding—is allocated in higher quantities to regions with higher demand and provision levels of public services. For example, ceteris paribus, regions with higher enrollment rates receive higher per capita recurrent allocations. At the same time, capital funding is equity-oriented in the sense that regions that are more "backward," with lower public service provision levels, are favored in the allocations so that they have the means to advance by accelerating their production of the appropriate types of capital stock. In addition, adjustments are made to the total (recurrent plus capital) allocations to adjust for intra-regional differences in revenue-raising ability, and to take into account economies of scale as well as higher unit provision costs in more sparsely populated regions. More details on this approach are given in Appendix B.

The "fiscal equalization" approach is being phased in gradually. The allocated Federal transfer to each region in the 2007/08 budget has been derived by calculating the weighted average of: (i) the allocation to that region as computed by the new "fiscal equalization" approach; and (ii) the allocation that would prevail if that region were to obtain the same share of the total transfers (to all regions combined) in 2007/08 as it did in 2006/07. The weights given to these two elements are 25 percent and 75 percent respectively. In short, the 2007/08 allocations give a weight of 25 percent to the new "fiscal equalization" approach and a weight of 75 percent to the old approach that was based on the "three-parameter" formula.

Similar calculations will be made to compute the allocations to regions in 2008/09, 2009/10, and 2010/11, except that the weight given to the "fiscal equalization" approach will rise successively from 25 percent in 2007/08 to 50 percent in 2008/09, then to 75 percent in 2009/10, and then to 100 percent in 2010/11. From 2010/11 onwards, the allocations will thus be based fully on the "fiscal equalization" approach.

Table 3.3 lists the share of total allocated Federal transfers going to each region in 2007/08, under the hypothetical scenario where the allocations are made purely according to the "fiscal equalization" approach. Also listed are the shares going to each region in the 2006/07 budget; these were allocated according to the old "three-parameter"-based approach. Finally, the table also provides figures on the population share of each region. The table illustrates the in-built bias of the old "three-parameter"-based approach against the smaller regions. The 2006/07 budget allocated a share of total transfers to each of the two smallest regions—Gambella and Harari—that was several times larger than their population share. If the allocations were based entirely on the new "fiscal equalization" approach, then the shares of the total pool of resources going to the smaller regions would be significantly lower, as the right-hand column of the table shows. However, these shares would still be larger than the population shares of the smaller regions, to an extent justified by economies of scale.

Table 3.3. Two Different Approaches for Allocating Federal Resources to Regions

	Population Share of Each Region in 2007/08	Share of Total Federal Transfers Going to Each Region in 2006/07 Budget	Share of Total Federal Transfers Going to Each Region in 2007/08 If New "Fiscal Equalization" Formula Was Fully Applied
Tigray	6.04%	7.58%	6.38%
Afar	1.96%	3.81%	2.51%
Amhara	26.59%	23.16%	26.49%
Oromyia	36.76%	32.25%	33.72%
Somali	6.02%	6.72%	6.68%
Benshangul-Gumuz	0.87%	2.62%	1.42%
SNNP	20.62%	19.13%	20.72%
Gambella	0.34%	1.92%	0.92%
Harari	0.26%	1.24%	0.50%
Diredawa	0.54%	1.56%	0.66%

Note: The 2006/07 shares are calculated from figures that include transfers from Treasury sources as well as from external loans and assistance (grants). Addis Ababa is excluded from the table, since it is mostly self-sufficient and does not receive any block grant transfer from Treasury sources.
Source: MoFED and Ethiopia House of Federation (2007).

Fiscal Transfers from Regions to Woredas

With the decentralization to local governments in 2002, block grants to local governments were introduced in four regions: Amhara, Oromiya, SNNPR, and Tigray (Figure 3.3), with

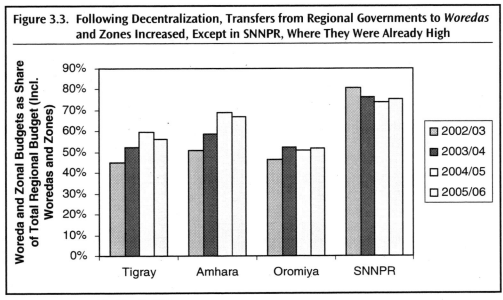

Figure 3.3. Following Decentralization, Transfers from Regional Governments to *Woredas* and Zones Increased, Except in SNNPR, Where They Were Already High

Source: Data provided by MoFED.

other regions soon following suit. The aim was to replace the incremental budget alloca-tion method with a transparent general purpose grant that gives autonomy to local gov-ernments. Initially after 2002, to make block grant allocations from regions to *woredas*, regions adopted the "three-parameter" formula used at the time for Federal block grant allocations to the regions, sometimes with some minor modifications. In this formula, block grants were allocated to each *woreda* on the basis of population, development level, and revenue collection effort.

In many regions, urban administrations with *woreda* status were created as indepen-dent administrative units two years or more after the start of *woreda*-level decentralization. In the initial stages of decentralization to *woredas*, most urban administrations did not exist as separate administrative entities; they were a part of larger *woredas* that incorporated the urban areas (towns) as well as surrounding rural areas. Around 2004 many towns were sep-arated from their "parent" *woredas* and given the status of urban administrations with sep-arate administrative boundaries and with *woreda* status. They are often subject to different rules than other (rural) *woredas*, as discussed below.

While some regions have continued to use the "three-parameter" formula for making block grant allocations to rural *woredas*,[2] others have experimented with different approaches. One advantage of Ethiopia's decentralized system is that regions are allowed to choose their own approach for making block grant allocations, as long as this is done in a non-discretionary, formula-based manner.

---

2. For most regions (with exceptions such as SNNPR), the discussion in this section applies to rural *woredas* only, and not to urban administrations. See below for a discussion of transfers to urban administrations.

SNNPR pioneered the "unit cost" approach for making block grant transfers to *woredas*. It used the "three-parameter" approach in 2002/03, the first year of decentralization to the *woreda*-level, but began using the "unit cost" approach from 2003/04 onwards. This is primarily a "needs-based" approach, and is similar in some ways to the "fiscal equalization" approach, which is one of the distribution methods currently under consideration for the Federal block allocations to the regions. As in the case of the "fiscal equalization" approach, SNNPR's "unit cost" approach allocates recurrent funding—which accounts for the bulk of total funding—to *woredas* in a "needs-based" manner, with higher per capita recurrent allocations generally going to *woredas* with higher per capita public service provision levels. More details are given in Box 3.1 and Appendix B, which explains some of the similarities and differences between SNNPR's "unit cost" approach and the "fiscal equalization" approach.

SNNPR's "unit cost" approach has received favorable reviews, and several other regions have subsequently also adopted it, or have been considering adopting it. Oromiya began decentralization to the *woreda*-level with the "three-parameter" approach in 2002/03, and continued until 2004/05. But from 2005/06 onwards, it decided to adopt the "unit cost" approach. Amhara also has now adopted the "unit cost" approach. Benshangul-Gumuz has been experimenting with a type of approach modeled very closely on the "fiscal equalization" approach being phased in for Federal block grant allocations.

Within SNNPR, the region's innovative switch to the "unit cost" approach in 2003/04 was not favored by all parties. When introduced, the move was justified internally on the grounds that it would be temporary and subject to revision as needed within a few years. The political climate favored a modification of the existing "unit cost" approach in 2006/07, and the region now uses a two-step approach to distribute block grants. First, block grants are allocated by the region to the zones using the "three-parameter" formula (giving weights of 60 percent, 25 percent, and 15 percent to the population, development index, and revenue effort of each zone, respectively). Next, each zone allocates block grants to the *woredas* within that zone, using a formula of its own choosing—with most using the "unit cost" approach to make this allocation. The involvement of the zones in the new system of allocating block grants is in recognition of the high degree of ethnic diversity in SNNPR, with each zone representing one ethnic group, or a small number of ethnic groups.

In several regions, urban administrations are not treated like other (rural) *woredas* in the block grant allocation process and are subject to different rules when determining transfer amounts from regions, even though they officially have *woreda* status.

Urban administrations perform "state functions" as well as "municipal functions." The "state functions" are financed by transfers from the regions and are similar to the functions performed by the rural *woredas*. The amount of the transfer in most regions is determined on an ad hoc basis, primarily to finance the recurrent costs of education, health, and other sectors. Recurrent needs are identified based on on-going expenditure obligations and the total transfer amount is negotiated with the region—in contrast to the formula-based approach used for block grant transfers to rural *woredas*.

However, there are differences in approach. In some regions such as SNNPR, the "state functions" of the urban administrations are financed by block grant transfers following a similar formula as for the rural *woredas*. In SNNPR, however, the transfers for the urban administrations come from a separate pool of funding, which is divided across the 19 different urban administrations in the region. In making budget allocations, the region independently decides how much funding to allocate the pool for the urban administrations,

Box 3.1. The "Unit Cost" Approach to Block Grant Allocation

Concerns with the "three-parameter" formula for allocating block grant resources, including the inability of many districts to meet their expenditure needs, the poor understanding of the formula by many, and the poor quality of information on which to base allocations, led SNNPR to try out the "unit cost" approach to make allocations, starting from 2003/04. The approach was used for block grant allocations to rural *woredas* as well as to urban administrations, but allocations for each of these came from a different "pool" (see Appendix B for full details on all this). Although many deemed the "unit cost" approach successful, a new hybrid approach was introduced in 2006/07, for reasons explained elsewhere in this section.

To implement the "unit cost" approach, SNNPR's Bureau of Finance and Economic Development would initially split the total envelope for block grant allocations to *woredas* (rural *woredas* or urban administrations) into two parts: (I) one allocated in a "needs-based" manner in line with *woredas'* recurrent needs (this accounted for the bulk of the total funding); and (II) one allocated in an equity-based manner for *woredas'* capital investment needs. From (I), the aim was to provide higher per capita funding levels to *woredas* with well-developed services so that they could have sufficient staff and operational budgets for efficient functioning. By contrast, from (II), the aim was to provide higher per capita allocations to *woredas* with *low* levels of public service–related infrastructure (for example, number of schools and health posts), enabling them to expand services through accelerated investment. The split between capital and recurrent parts of the envelope was based on historical information and subject to annual revision.

Recurrent allocations were based on specific performance targets for each subsector for the following fiscal year (number of primary students to be enrolled, number of health posts to be managed). Starting from 2004/05, these targets were set as part of "performance agreements" signed between *woredas* and the region, whereby the *woreda* commits to attain the targets (see Box 3.2 on performance agreements in SNNPR). Recurrent funding allocations for each sub-sector, for each *woreda,* were calculated from these performance targets as well as target values for "cost drivers," or key measures determining unit cost. For example, each *woreda's* recurrent allocation for primary education was based on its expected primary enrollment as well as an explicitly stated target value for each of the following cost drivers, among others: (i) the pupil-teacher ratio (PTR) in the *woreda;* (ii) the average teacher salary in the *woreda.* The target values for these cost drivers were allowed to differ across *woredas,* in recognition of past patterns, but they were expected to converge over time to the national average, for each cost driver—leading, over time, to a convergence across *woredas* of unit costs (for example, of per student primary spending in the case of the primary education subsector).

For example, if a *woreda* had a PTR that is lower than the national average in any one fiscal year, then the target PTR assigned to it in the following fiscal year's recurrent allocation process would be higher than in the current year, but lower than the national average. The aim was to equalize *woreda* PTRs as well as other cost drivers across *woredas* over time.

Ultimately, each *woreda's* total allocation was transferred as a block grant and it was free to use this funding as it wished, the only expectation being that it should meet the performance targets (such as for primary enrollment) that it had signed on to in the performance agreements. It was not obliged to meet the targets for the cost drivers (except when required by the performance agreement—see Appendix B). However, these cost-driver targets were explicitly stated and in practice each *woreda* had an incentive to try and meet them, regardless. In the case of its target PTR, for example, a *woreda* was free to hire more than the number of teachers that was implied by its target PTR, but doing so would require it to dig into funding allocated by the formula for other uses. This was unlikely to happen since most *woredas* tended to be strapped for resources.

Box 3.2. Performance Agreements in SNNPR

From 2003/04 to 2005/06, SNNPR used the "unit cost" approach to make block grant allocations to *woredas* (see Box 3.1). In 2004/05 and 2005/06, SNNPR signed annual "performance
agreements" with *woredas*. In these agreements, *woredas* would commit to attaining specified
numerical performance targets in each key sector, in the following fiscal year. The calculation
of the *woreda*'s block grant allocation for the following fiscal year would, in turn, be based on
these agreed-to performance targets.

For example, key performance targets in the primary education subsector were primary enrollment and the number of new schools to be constructed. Each *woreda* would agree to attain specific numerical targets for each of these, and would receive funding allocations accordingly.

One difficulty encountered by the region was how to ensure that *woredas* adhered to their
performance agreements. One approach used to encourage adherence was to publicize the
names of the *woredas* who had performed poorly, as well as those who had performed well,
with regard to the performance agreements. Regional officials also stated that they had been
looking into ways of implementing a legal framework to enforce the agreements.

SNNPR has now switched to a two-step process where the region allocates block grants to
zones, and each zone then allocates block grants to *woredas* (see above). A new system of performance agreements is being established, whereby the region signs performance agreements
with the zones, and each zone signs agreements with its *woredas*.

---

and how much to the pool for the rural *woredas*. The result is that there may have been
some differential treatment of urban administrations as compared to rural *woredas*, which
the region has justified by pointing to urban-rural differences in the prices of goods and
services and in the costs of living, among other things.

The municipal functions of urban administrations everywhere are financed exclusively
from local revenues (through taxes, including land lease income, fees, and user charges).
Municipal functions receive no regular financial support from higher levels of government.
There are also municipalities without the status of urban administrations, which may raise
their own revenues to perform municipal functions. These do not perform "state" functions, and do not receive any revenues from higher-level governments; also, there is no tax-
sharing program with municipalities.

Woredas sometimes receive financial assistance from specific donor or NGO projects;
from federal grants, such as the Road Fund, the Food Security Program, and the Public
Sector Capacity Building Program; and from contingency assistance, selected cash transfers and asset transfers from the region. These fund flows—some of which are off-budget—
are often highly unpredictable and arbitrary.

The share of regional budgets allocated to the *woredas* varies across regions, ranging
from 52 to 81 percent (Table 3.4). Allocations also vary across sectors and sub-sectors, and
also across and within regions.

In 2002/03, 46 percent of the regional budget in Oromiya was allocated to the *woredas*;
50 percent of the total treasury and regional budget went to regional and zonal sector bureaus
(Table 3.5). The situation changed in 2002/03 and 2004/05, when the shares of the budget
going to *woredas* increased to 51 percent. The significant portion of the recurrent budgets
allocated to social services (for example, health and education) reflects mainly teacher
salaries.

Box 3.3. Devolution of Power in Theory and in Practice

Government decentralization is a trend that is happening around the world. Yet, in many countries, practice often does not follow theory, and there is often less real decentralization on the ground than there should be according to a country's legal framework. This is partly because implementation takes time, partly because there is resistance from certain segments of society, and sometimes because the capacity to take on new functions or responsibilities may not exist. Although Ethiopia has made great strides in implementing real decentralization of power to lower-level governments, this has occurred in some spheres more than in others.

Overall, regions appear to have a large amount of autonomy and decisionmaking power. One manifestation of this is that regions are allowed to determine what formula to use to distribute block grant resources across *woredas*. The only constraint is that these resources are expected to be allocated in a rules-based and non-discretionary manner, following a predetermined formula or set of clear, quantitative criteria. As a result, different regions have adopted different approaches for distributing block grant resources, effectively carrying out a "natural experiment" that enables a comparison of the effectiveness of different approaches (see Chapter 4).

At the *woreda* level, many argue that there is much less autonomy and decisionmaking power. This statement is difficult to prove conclusively and opposing arguments can certainly be made. But support for the statement comes from two recent studies:

♦ According to a report by Oxfam (see Adal 2005), *woreda* decisions are often largely based on "sectoral guidelines from regions and party leadership", and plans are based more on "regional targets" than on "community needs".

♦ According to a World Bank (2005d) study on empowerment in Ethiopia, local government officials have an "upward view for inputs into decisionmaking and accountability", looking "toward their political parties or horizontally toward officials in the state bureaucracy for decisionmaking guidance".

According to the World Bank study, this continued reliance on higher levels of government can be explained, in part, by low capacity on the part of *woreda* officials. If this argument is accepted, then autonomy and decisionmaking powers on the part of *woreda* administrations can be expected to improve over time, as capacity at the lower levels improves. It should not be forgotten that decentralization to the *woreda* level only began in 2002/03, and the experience of many countries shows it takes time for true autonomy to take hold at the lower levels after decentralization has begun. By contrast, decentralization to the regions began with a big push in 1993/94.

Trends in Regional Spending and Regional Revenues

The devolution of expenditure responsibilities started in 1993/94 with a big push, when 45 percent of the overall government budget was transferred to the regions. Since then, regional spending has been growing at an annual average of 13 percent (see Table 3.7), with a slowdown in the late 1990's during the conflict. The recurrent budget tripled in ten years, from 2.3 billion to 7.9 billion and now accounts for 72 percent of the regional budget. Regions are major implementers of primary service delivery programs and currently manage about 80 percent of the pro-poor recurrent budget.

Federally mandated programs that are financed from Special Purpose Grants (SPGs)—including the Food Security, Productive Safety Net, PSCAP and HIV/AIDS programs—are in fact executed by regional administrations, even though they officially appear only in the Federal budget. The SPGs account for about 21 percent of total regional spending, if the latter is

Table 3.4.   Regional Budgets and Share of Budgets Transferred to *Woredas* in Four Regions, 2005/06

	Regional budget (including *woreda-level budgets*), in million Birr				*Woreda* share of regional budget, in percent			
	Tigray	Amhara	Oromiya	SNNPR	Tigray	Amhara	Oromiya	SNNPR
Administration & Gen. Serv.	168.9	447.8	648.6	472.2	67.8	60.1	61.9	81.2
Organ of the State	42.9	93.3	160.6	97.7	71.0	82.8	76.2	83.9
Justice	34.2	48.5	85.6	45.6	39.2	24.4	42.1	87.3
Public Order	36.3	148.5	176.4	100.1	76.7	49.5	42.0	90.5
General Service	29.7	106.5	150.1	129.2	71.7	80.3	66.8	87.4
Economic Services	165.8	573.7	912.2	365.8	51.3	57.9	27.4	68.5
Agriculture & Rural Development	90.2	381.0	489.5	268.7	63.3	75.1	46.4	82.5
Natural Resource	36.2	123.6	143.7	14.7	43.2	28.5	7.1	0.0
o/w Water	30.6	95.4	143.8	12.3	41.4	29.9	7.0	0.0
Construction	23.1	39.3	237.7	19.7	26.5	8.3	2.7	15.4
o/w Road Construction	9.9	27.1	134.8	12.9	58.5	9.4	1.4	0.0
o/w Urban Development	7.5	12.2	98.3	4.7	0.0	5.9	0.0	64.2

Social Services	425.6	953.8	1,534.6	794.8	61.6	75.8	63.0	87.3
Education	303.2	687.6	1,148.9	639.8	66.9	78.4	69.5	89.4
o/w Primary & Junior Education	205.9	363.4	441.5	425.3	86.9	100.0	96.4	99.0
o/w Secondary School Education	27.8	85.2	118.1	48.9	68.1	76.0	44.9	100.0
o/w Technical Education	12.9	36.0	92.9	31.3	19.9	0.0	0.0	0.0
o/w Higher Education	53.4	19.1	52.0	21.3	0.0	0.0	0.0	4.4
Health	107.9	228.9	300.3	149.2	50.0	71.9	40.1	80.3
o/w Prim. Health, Clinic & Hth Stations	50.5	122.0	81.7	97.5	92.8	91.7	68.1	88.1
o/w Hospitals	40.1	44.1	82.4	13.9	0.0	0.0	9.3	0.0
o/w Malaria Prevention	10.8	11.9	12.8	1.6	38.7	95.8	24.2	0.0
o/w Nurses Training	0.0	4.8	1.9	0.0	0.0	0.0	0.0	0.0
Social Affaires	3.1	7.2	0.0	1.5	9.8	25.7	0.0	0.3
DPPC	5.1	9.9	22.2	1.4	48.4	27.5	83.2	15.7
Food Security	*1.4*	*0.0*	*5.3*	*0.7*	*38.1*	*0.0*	*50.7*	*0.0*
HIV/AIDS Office	*1.3*	*1.3*	*1.2*	*4.5*	*65.4*	*60.1*	*0.0*	*100.0*
Miscellaneous	*78.1*	*159.1*	*15.0*	*72.1*	*58.1*	*66.0*	*0.0*	*75.0*
Total Recurrent and Capital Budget	**840.9**	**2,135.8**	**3,116.8**	**1,710.0**	**60.5**	**66.9**	**52.0**	**81.1**

Source: Data provided by MoFED.

Table 3.5. Block Grant Allocations in Oromiya, 2002/03–2004/05

Budget Source	2002/03		2003/04		2004/05	
	Million Birr	%	Million Birr	%	Million Birr	%
Woredas	1,045	46	1,260	51	1,384	51
Regional bureaus	1,138	50	1,176	47	1,285	47
Contingencies	81	4	45	2	38	2
Total	**2,264**	**100**	**2,482**	**100**	**2,707**	**100**

Source: Mussa (2005a).

Table 3.6. Block Grant Allocations in SNNPR, 2002/03–2004/05

Level	2002/03 (million Birr)	2003/04 (million Birr)	2004/05 (million Birr)
Rural *woredas*	901 (72%)	883 (64%)	931 (61%)
Zones	100 (9%)	98 (7%)	103 (7%)
Urban administrations	0.0	64 (5%)	120 (8%)
Regional bureaus	237 (19%)	320 (23%)	359 (24%)
Total	**1,239**	**1,366**	**1,514**

Source: Mussa (2005b).

defined as spending from regional budgets plus SPG-financed (and Federal-mandate) programs that are executed by regional governments.[3]

The magnitude of resources financed from SPGs in 2005/06 was about Birr 3.7 billion, of which the Food Security SPG accounts for more than half. Total resources handled by regional governments, including the SPG-financed programs, amounted to about Birr 16.9 billion. In the past three years, the total amount of SPG-financed spending increased substantially due to a doubling of Food Security grant funding as well as the implementation of the PSCAP and Productive Safety Net Programme SPGs (see Figure 3.4).

Regions are heavily reliant on transfers from the Federal government because of their limited share of total government revenues. Regions on average collect 18 percent of total consolidated government revenue (including Federal revenue), even though regional budgets in total are about 38 percent of the total consolidated (including the Federal) government budget. Figure 3.5 provides more details on the main sources of regional revenue.

Regions collect about half of all direct taxes, 15 percent of all indirect taxes, and 22 percent of all non-tax revenue. Among the direct taxes, regions collect 100 percent of taxes on agriculture income and capital gains, as well as of rural and urban land use fees.

Regarding regional revenues, one positive development has been a decline in the coefficient of variation[4] of regions' expenditure financed from own sources, from 0.69 in 2001/02 to 0.43 in 2005/06. This means that there is now less variation among the regions in the extent to which their expenditure is financed from own revenue sources. Contributory factors include improved revenue mobilization in poorer regions.

---

3. These figures and information, as well as some of the other information in this chapter, come from the informative World Bank study "Ethiopia: Review of Public Finance" (World Bank, 2006a).

4. The coefficient of variation is the standard deviation of a distribution divided by the mean of the distribution. It is a commonly used measure of variation.

Table 3.7. Trends in Regional Expenditure, 1993/4–2005/06

(In millions of Birr)	93/94–97/98 Pre-actual (annual average)	98/99–02/03 Pre-actual (annual average)	2002/03 Pre-actual	2003/04 Pre-actual	2004/05 Pre-actual	2005/06 Budget
Regional Government						
Recurrent Expenditure	2323.6	3726.5	4755.5	5794.8	6154.7	7914.7
Capital Expenditure[2]	1356.3	1673.3	1470.3	1918.2	2672.9	5173.7
Total Expenditure	3679.9	5399.8	6225.8	7713.0	8827.6	13088.4
Consolidated Government						
Recurrent Expenditure	5809.4	12091.9	13527.1	11960.8	13035.7	16001.3
Recurrent Expenditure (excl non-discretionary)[1]	3520.1	5530.1	7077.5	7730.4	8383.4	11030.4
Capital Expenditure[2]	3457.3	4836.8	6313.4	8271.6	11515.0	18697.3
Total Expenditure	9266.7	16928.6	19840.5	20232.4	24550.7	34698.7
Total Expenditure (excl. non-discretionary)	6977.3	10366.9	13390.9	16002.0	19898.4	29727.7
Regional Expenditures in percent of Consolidated Government Expenditures						
- Including Non-Discretionary						
Regional Share of Total Spending	39.7	31.9	31.4	38.1	36.0	37.7
Regional Share of Recurrent Spending	40.0	30.8	35.2	48.4	47.2	49.5
Regional Share of Capital Spending	39.2	34.6	23.3	23.2	23.2	27.7
- Excluding Non-Discretionary						
Regional Share of Total Spending	52.7	52.1	46.5	48.2	44.4	44.0
Regional Share of Recurrent Spending	66.0	67.4	67.2	75.0	73.4	71.8
Regional Share of Capital Spending	39.2	34.6	23.3	23.2	23.2	27.7

Notes:
1. Non-discretionary includes debt service, defense, and relief aid.
2. Pre-actuals for regional capital expenditure do not include external funds due to lack of reporting from regions until accounts are closed.
Source: Data provided by MoFED.

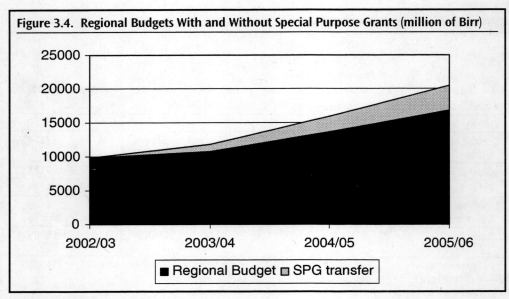

Figure 3.4. Regional Budgets With and Without Special Purpose Grants (million of Birr)

Source: Data provided by MoFED.

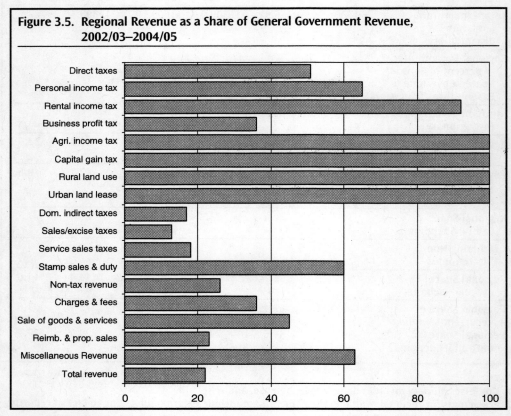

Figure 3.5. Regional Revenue as a Share of General Government Revenue, 2002/03–2004/05

Source: Data provided by MoFED.

Changes in Federal and Regional Spending on Education and Health

Real public per capita spending on education more than doubled between 2000 and 2005, from about Birr 30 to about Birr 65 (Figure 3.6). But much of this increase was due to the increase in federal expenditures, which reflected the rapid expansion in spending on tertiary education. Per capita education and health expenditures assigned to the regions and *woredas* have remained roughly constant since the decentralization to the *woreda*-level in 2002. Overall, over the last several years extending before 2002, the nominal rate of growth of total regional (including *woreda*) spending has been roughly in line with inflation, reflecting the relatively slow growth rate of the main revenue source for regions—Federal block grant transfers (Figure 3.1). This appears inadequate, given the regions' (and *woredas'*) responsibility for improving the access and quality of primary-level services.

Real education spending by subnational governments (excluding Addis Ababa), which are responsible for providing primary and secondary education, was 79 percent higher in 2004/05 than in 1997/97–1998/99. However, given the 127 percent increase in primary enrollment and the 134 percent increase in secondary enrollment, the increases were insufficient to maintain pupil-teacher or pupil-section (the number of students per class[5]) ratios, both of which rose.

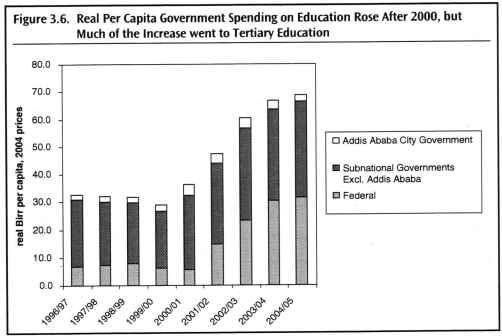

Figure 3.6. Real Per Capita Government Spending on Education Rose After 2000, but Much of the Increase went to Tertiary Education

Source: Data provided by MoFED.

---

    5. In Ethiopia as in many countries, students at each grade within a school are divided into one or more classes/sections. A class/section is a group of students who sit together and together undergo instruction in all core subjects. A "class" is not quite the same as a "classroom," although in most cases a school would need to have at least one classroom for each class/section.

With resources increasing at a slower pace than enrollment and the real wages of teach-ers rising, the pupil-teacher ratio rose from 42:1 in 1996/97 to 66:1 in 2004/05 at the primary level and from 36:1 to 58:1 at the secondary level. Over the same period, pupil-section ratios rose from 57:1 to 69:1 at the primary level and from 66:1 to 93:1 at the secondary level. These ratios are very high by international standards.

In the health sector, real spending at the subnational level over the past several years rose by less than the increase in the population, resulting in a decline in real per capita health spending at this level (Figure 3.7). Real health spending by subnational governments excluding Addis Ababa rose about 13 percent in 2004/05 relative to 1996/97–1998/99. Over the same period, the population increased by about 17 percent, resulting in a slight decline in real per capita health spending at this level, from Birr 10.1 to Birr 9.7.

This slight decline in real per-capita health spending on the part of subnational gov-ernments needs to be evaluated alongside the very significant growth in public health spending on basic services that has taken place via channels outside of subnational gov-ernment budgets. The amount of off-budget spending on basic health services (for exam-ple, local provision by NGOs) has grown substantially over the last few years, as has the quantity of goods that are procured and paid for centrally but distributed at the local level. Nevertheless, as in the case of education, the trend in real per-capita subnational spending on health appears to reflect an inadequate growth rate in Federal block grant transfers to the regions, in the face of growing regional commitments to basic service delivery. This is likely to change over the next few years, if the Federal government fulfils its commitments to substantially increase block grant transfers to the regions (see Chapter 5).

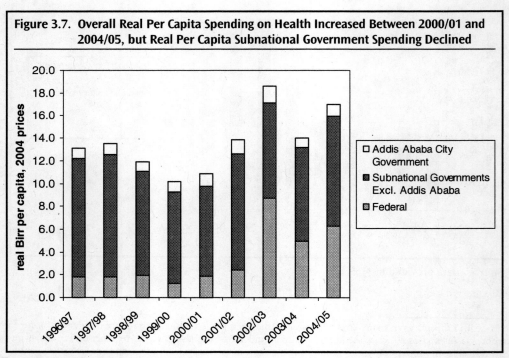

Figure 3.7. **Overall Real Per Capita Spending on Health Increased Between 2000/01 and 2004/05, but Real Per Capita Subnational Government Spending Declined**

Source: Data provided by MoFED.

Performance of Regional Budgets

Regional government revenue tends to be unpredictable with a volatile performance record across years (see Table 3.8). On average over the past three years, regions' actual revenue fell short of plans by more than ten percent. In FY2004/05, regions managed to collect only 71 percent of their planned revenue. In particular in Addis Ababa, non-tax (mainly lease) revenue fell short by more than 50 percent. Excluding Addis Ababa, the rest of the regions managed to collect 81 percent of planned revenue in 2004/05.

It is not surprising that recurrent spending is more predictable than capital spending. The former comprises predominantly wage and salaries and actual regional spending has been close to budgeted levels, even better than the general government. In the three of the four years under consideration, actual regional spending was more than 90 percent of their budgeted levels. However, under-spending of the capital budget at the regional level is a major concern, especially for funding from non-Treasury sources (project-specific donor funding).

Table 3.8. Aggregate Fiscal Performance (in percent of budget)				
	2001/02	**2002/03**	**2003/04**	**2004/05**
Revenue (domestic)				
General government	82	88	96	87
Regional government	76	85	83	71
Recurrent expenditure				
General government	85	104	86	90
Regional government	98	87	93	95
Capital expenditure				
General government	79	92	92	90
Regional government	61	49	55	52
Treasury source only (regional governments)	95	93	75	65

Note: The "General Government" refers to the combined Federal and regional governments.
Source: Data from MoFED.

The Structure of Woreda-Level Budgets

Responsibility for social service delivery has been devolved to *woredas* with education (predominantly primary) being the single most devolved category of sector expenditure. In the 2005/06 budgets for the four main decentralizing regions (see Figure 3.8), *woredas* administer 81 percent of the regional education recurrent budget, while the ratio for health is about 65 percent. The pace of devolution varies across sectors, as the figure shows.

On average, capital spending accounts for only 16 percent of the district-level budgets. Shares of the capital budgets accounted for by *woredas* by sector vary from 11 percent for education to 27 percent for the economic sectors, for the four main decentralizing regions (FDRs—Amhara, Oromiya, SNNPR, and Tigray).

The *woreda*-level budget is dominated by wage and salary costs, which account for about 78 percent of total recurrent spending in the FDRs. *Woredas* are facing increasing

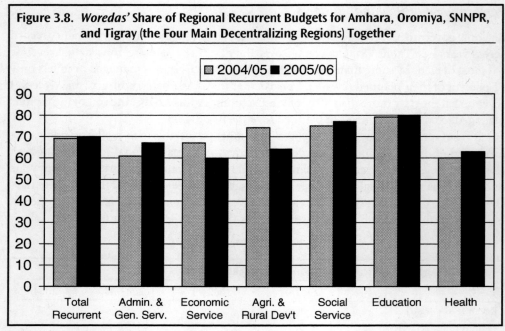

Figure 3.8. *Woredas'* Share of Regional Recurrent Budgets for Amhara, Oromiya, SNNPR, and Tigray (the Four Main Decentralizing Regions) Together

Source: Data provided by MOFED.

pressure from the fast-growing wage bill. Indeed, in the FDRs, the budget for salary and allowances rose by 33 percent in 2005/06 compared to an increase in the overall *woreda* budget of 17 percent. As a result, district-level budgets for operational (non-personnel) spending fell in absolute terms (by Birr 50 million) as well as in relative terms.

The decline in operating budgets and the pattern of accelerating wage bills is not uniform across sectors. The education sector has been the most affected with the wage share rising from 70 percent in 2004/05 to 92 percent in 2005/06 in the FDRs. For the rest of the sectors, the increase in wage share ranges from 2 to 3 percent only.

CHAPTER 4

How Did Decentralization to *Woreda* Level Affect the Delivery of Social Services?

This chapter examines the implementation of decentralization to the *woreda* level in two of the largest regions in Ethiopia, SSNPR and Oromiya. The two regions' 39 million people represent roughly 55 percent of the country's population. One benefit of decentralization and devolution of power to the regions is that the regions are allowed to determine the formula and criteria used to distribute block grant resources to *woredas*, with the constraint that these resources are expected to be distributed in a rules-based, objective manner. As a result, different regions have adopted different approaches for distributing block grant resources, effectively carrying out a "natural experiment" that enables a comparison of the effectiveness of different approaches. One of the reasons for choosing SNNPR and Oromiya for the analysis is to examine the impact of two contrasting methods of block grants allocations—until the fiscal year 2005/06 the former used the "unit cost" approach while the latter used the original "three-parameter" approach until the year 2004/05. (See Chapter 3 for a description of both approaches.[6])

The report team obtained longitudinal data on budgets and expenditures as well as outcomes and inputs in education and health at the *woreda* level. Data were obtained before decentralization (2001) and after decentralization (2004) for all 123 *woredas* (including urban administrations) in SNNPR and 69 of the 197 *woredas* (including urban administrations) in Oromiya.[7] Indicators of socioeconomic situation were created, based on population,

---

6. As Chapter 3 notes, several regions treat urban administrations differently from other *woredas*. SNNPR's "unit cost" approach was used to determine block grant allocations to urban administrations, but these came from a different "pool" than that used to distribute block grant resources to rural *woredas*. In Oromiya, however, urban administrations have been treated in the same manner as other *woredas* with allocations for both coming from the same pool.

7. These figures correspond to the situation in 2004. The total number of *woredas* is now more than 123 in SNNPR and more than 197 in Oromiya, due to the creation of new *woredas* (via the splitting of existing *woredas*)—see below for more on this.

agricultural and animal production, pastoral areas, food security status, physical infrastructure, area, urbanization, and distance to main urban centers. School-level scores on Grade 8 examinations were obtained for the two periods. Because of the limitations in the data, the analysis could be conducted more extensively for SNNPR than for Oromiya, and more for education rather than health services.

The expenditure data obtained represent expenditures from Treasury sources only, and appearing in *woreda* budgets. The following are not captured by the present dataset: (i) *woreda* on-budget spending funded directly from foreign assistance and loans; (ii) off-budget spending; (iii) spending by zones and by the regional government itself; and (iv) *woreda* spending funded from special-purpose Federal grants or SPGs (for example, PSCAP, Food Security Program and Productive Safety Nets Program grants). These data gaps are recognized as limitations to the present analysis.

The omission of the SPGs from the expenditure data is not likely to significantly affect the results of the current analysis. In 2001, total SPG funding was almost zero. In 2004, before a large acceleration in the growth of SPG funding, the main SPGs were PSCAP (mainly for capacity building at the district level); anti-HIV/AIDS grants; and Food Security Program (FSP) grants.[8] Of these, the latter—totaling 1 billion Birr—accounted for the bulk of the total, and funded mainly agricultural packages for households as well as resettlements with a small amount going to other related activities; it did not provide cash transfers. Thus, there is unlikely to have been much "leakage" of FSP or other SPG funds to education or health expenditures.[9]

One difficulty with quantitative comparisons of the pre- and post-decentralization periods of analysis (2001 and 2004) is that there were many cases where a *woreda* split into two or even three—thus creating one or even two new localities with separate administrative boundaries. Each of these new localities became a new *woreda*—either a rural *woreda* or an urban administration with *woreda* status; urban administrations did not exist before decentralization to the *woreda* level. For consistency, all comparisons between 2001 and 2004 of expenditure or outcome measures were done using either: (i) pre-decentralization *woreda* boundaries for both periods of time, or (ii) post-decentralization boundaries for both time periods. The former approach, for example, treats all newly created *woreda*s in 2004 as a part of the original *woreda*s to which they belonged, rather than as separate units. More details on this and other technical aspects are given in Appendix E.

Increases in *Woreda*-Level Spending Following Decentralization

Did decentralization[10] change expenditure patterns at the *woreda* level? *Woreda* expenditures capture virtually all government spending on primary service delivery (primary education and health) both before and after decentralization. Spending from donor and NGO sources which are not flowing through the *woreda* budget are not available and thus not

---

8. The Productive Safety Net Program (PSNP) is currently a major SPG program, but it began only in 2005.

9. Some "leakage" could still have occurred. For some household beneficiaries of the FSP, FSP expenditure on in-kind items for the household could have displaced private household funds (from household income) that would otherwise have gone towards purchase of these same items. Some private household funds would have been freed up, and some of this could have gone towards education or health expenditures.

10. Only recurrent expenditures are examined, as capital spending did not go through *woreda* budgets before decentralization (it was funded through zonal budgets).

captured in this analysis. Before decentralization, spending on primary service delivery went through *woreda* budgets even though *woredas* had no control over the amount or composition of this spending.

Recurrent expenditure by *woreda* administrations rose significantly with decentralization (Figure 4.1). Mean recurrent expenditure nearly doubled between 2001 and 2004, in both SNNPR and Oromiya. A means test of expenditure per capita suggests that decentralization significantly changed public expenditure at the *woreda* level, as a result of: (i) the transfer to *woredas* of some functional responsibilities; (ii) much higher *woreda* administrative spending to enable *woreda* administrations to handle their new responsibilities; and (iii) an increase in

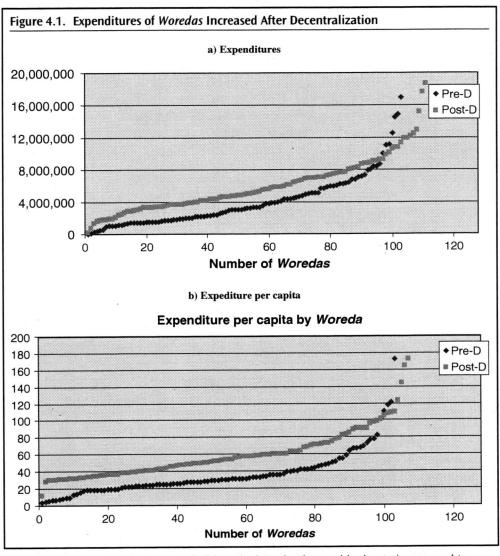

Figure 4.1. Expenditures of *Woredas* Increased After Decentralization

a) Expenditures

b) Expediture per capita

Expenditure per capita by *Woreda*

Note: "Pre-decentralization boundaries" (see the introduction to this chapter) were used to calculate all expenditure figures for the above and other diagrams.
Source of data: SNNPR Bureau of Finance and Economic Development (BOFED).

per capita recurrent spending on some items that had been going through *woreda* budgets before decentralization.

In terms of sectoral allocation, *woredas* have consistently allocated the largest shares of their budgets to education and health, which accounted for almost 55 percent of their budgets in 2004 (41 percent to education and 12 percent to health on average in SNNPR; 45 percent to education and 9 percent to health on average in Oromiya). In SNNPR *woredas,* per capita spending rose in all sectors between 2001 and 2004 (Figure 4.2). Recurrent spending on primary education, which represented more than 85 percent of recurrent spending on education before decentralization, rose to 90 percent of education expenditures, suggesting the importance of basic education in resource allocation (Figure 4.3). Per capita health spending rose following decentralization, although it remains low.

Decentralization Appears to Have Improved the Distribution of Expenditures Across *Woredas* with Worse-off *Woredas* Benefiting the Most

The increase in spending on education and health was accompanied by a narrowing of the differences in per capita spending across *woredas* in both SNNPR and Oromiya (Tables 4.1 and 4.2). At the same time, the differences in per student education spending across *woredas* also narrowed in both regions. The decline in the coefficient of variation for most of the spend-

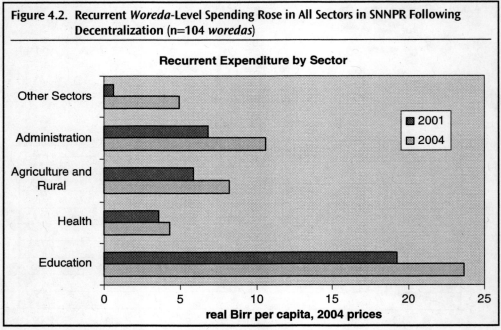

Figure 4.2. Recurrent *Woreda*-Level Spending Rose in All Sectors in SNNPR Following Decentralization (n=104 *woredas*)

Note: All calculations regarding expenditures, in all the diagrams, were done using "pre-decentralization boundaries" (see the introduction to this chapter). This explains why there are 104 *woredas* in total rather than 123 (which would be the case if "post-decentralization" boundaries were used).

Source of data: SNNPR BOFED.

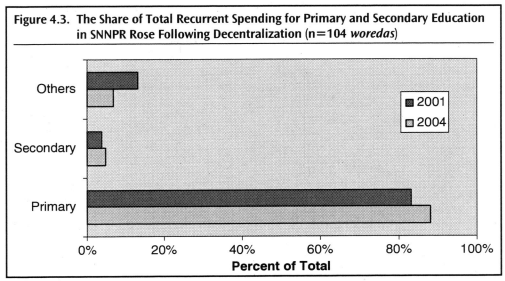

Figure 4.3. The Share of Total Recurrent Spending for Primary and Secondary Education in SNNPR Rose Following Decentralization (n=104 *woredas*)

Note: Calculations assume "pre-decentralization" *woreda* boundaries.
Source of data: SNNPR BOFED.

ing measures suggests that per capita health spending and per student education spending in many lagging *woredas* are catching up with that in better off *woredas*. (Unlike the standard deviation or variance, the coefficient of variation is comparable across distributions and is thus the appropriate variability measure to use here. See Appendix E for more details.)

There is generally more variability in the spending measures among the SNNPR *woredas* than in the Oromiya *woredas* in the sample. This reflects the fact that there is much less variability within the Oromiya sample than within the SNNPR group of *woredas* to begin with, in characteristics such as extent of food insecurity and whether or not a *woreda* is pastoral. Indeed, unlike the SNNPR sample, the Oromiya sample does not have any pastoral *woredas*.

The narrowing in the dispersion of various spending measures after decentralization (Tables 4.1 and 4.2) is likely attributable to the equalization effects that can be attained through formula-based allocation of resources through block grants. They mirror the experience of countries around the world, that formula-based allocations are typically fairer than arbitrary or ad hoc allocations. As described earlier, until the fiscal year 2005/06, SNNPR uses the "unit cost" approach for block grant allocations while Oromiya used the "three-parameter" approach until 2004/05. In the longer run, the "unit cost" approach tends to equalize per student spending across *woredas* (see Box 3.1), while the "three-parameter" approach tends to equalize per capita spending across *woredas* (because the bulk of the funding is allocated in proportion to *woreda* population). In the first two years since decentralization to *woredas* was introduced in 2003, the data show that both these types of equalization have occurred for several education-spending measures in SNNPR and Oromiya. This implies that the distribution of funding across *woredas* in the two regions was highly unequal to begin with, before decentralization when the allocations were made on an ad hoc basis. The differences between the unit cost approach and the three-parameter approach are explained in detail in Appendix A and Appendix B.

Table 4.1. *Woreda*-Level Spending on Education and Health in SNNPR, by Category of Spending, 2001 and 2004 (n=104 *woredas*, 2004 Birr prices)

Spending Category	Mean Spending 2001	Mean Spending 2004	Coefficient of Variation 2001[2]	Coefficient of Variation 2004[2]
Recurrent primary education per primary student[3]	121	143	0.52	0.41
Total recurrent education per student[4]	140	157	0.44	0.36
Recurrent primary education per capita	16.0	20.8	0.56	0.41
Total recurrent education per capita	19.3	23.7	0.61	0.54
Recurrent health per capita	3.58	4.25	1.08	0.63

Notes:
1. Calculations assume "pre-decentralization" *woreda* boundaries.
2. All pastoral *woredas* were excluded from the calculations for the coefficients of variation, since they are very different from other *woredas*, for the following reasons: (i) they have very low population densities and therefore high unit costs (low pupil-section and pupil-teacher ratios); (ii) teachers in pastoral *woredas* earn a 40 percent increment over their base salaries as a hardship allowance; (iii) there is a special fund providing additional resources just to the pastoral *woredas*. When the coefficients of variation were calculated for pastoral *woredas*, they fell between 2001 and 2004 for all spending measures, as is the case for the non-pastoral *woredas* (reported in the table).
3. Only includes students in public primary schools.
4. This measure incorporates both primary and lower secondary school recurrent spending (i.e. for Grades 9 and 10); its denominator is the total number of primary and lower secondary school students. Note that this measure is not entirely comparable between 2001 and 2004, because there has not always been consistency on the question of which government level (*woreda*, zone or region) funds lower secondary schooling in a locality. The difficulty arises in part because there are many "combination schools" with both lower and upper secondary schooling, and often with teachers teaching at both levels. *Woredas* are supposed to be responsible in principle for lower secondary schooling, and the region for upper secondary schooling. But at the "combination schools," it is difficult to ensure that each level of government funds (from its own budget) only the type of schooling for which it is officially responsible. By contrast, funding for all public primary schools consistently passed through *woreda* budgets only in 2001 as well as in 2004.
Source of data: SNNPR BOFED and SNNPR Bureau of Education.

Increase in Spending in Remote, Pastoral, and Food-Insecure Woredas

Decentralization in SNNPR disproportionately favored remote (more than 50 kilometers from a zonal capital), food-insecure, and pastoral *woreda*s (Tables 4.3 to 4.5). The aggregate budget for education, for example, rose 36 percent in remote *woreda*s and just 3 percent in *woreda*s located less than 50 kilometers from a zonal capital. A similar trend occurred for health. Aggregate spending on education and health by pastoral *woreda*s rose by 57–75 percent between 2001 and 2004, while spending by non-pastoral *woreda*s rose by just 9–16 percent. Remote *woreda*s also gained disproportionately from decentralization, with per student expenditures for primary education rising about 20 percent as opposed to just 16 percent for non-remote *woreda*s. The percentage change in per student secondary expenditure exceeded 95 percent in remote and food-insecure *woreda*s, while it was just 49 percent in non-remote *woreda*s and just 4 percent in food-secure *woreda*s.

Table 4.2. *Woreda*-Level Per Capita Spending on Education and Health in Oromiya, by Category of Spending, 2001 and 2004 (n=69 *woredas,* 2004 Birr prices)

Spending Category	Mean Spending 2001	Mean Spending 2004	Coefficient of Variation 2001	Coefficient of Variation 2004
Recurrent primary education per primary student	132	149	0.47	0.30
Total recurrent education per student	154	163	0.52	0.32
Recurrent primary education per capita	14.1	20.3	0.53	0.41
Total recurrent education per capita	17.2	23.3	0.63	0.45
Recurrent health per capita	2.77	3.28	1.34	0.58

Notes: Calculations assume "pre-decentralization" *woreda* boundaries. The sample for Oromiya did not have any pastoral *woredas* (see footnote 2 of previous table). See also other notes of previous table, which also apply here.
Source of data: Oromiya BOFED and Oromiya Bureau of Education.

Table 4.3. *Woreda*-Level Spending on Education and Health in SNNPR, by Type of *Woreda*, 2001 and 2004 (n=104 *woredas*)
(real thousands of Birr, 2004 prices)

Type of *Woreda*	Education			Health		
	2001 Total Budget (average across all *woredas*)	2004 Total Budget (average across all *woredas*)	Percent Change	2001 Total Budget (average across all *woredas*)	2004 Total Budget (average across all *woredas*)	Percent Change
Remote (more than 50 kilometers from a zonal capital)	1,897	2,576	36	314	398	27
Nonremote (less than 50 kilometers from a zonal capital)	3,681	3,778	3	501	512	2
Food insecure	3,073	3,760	22	453	503	11
Food secure	2,051	2,283	11	346	393	14
Pastoral	897	1,574	75	253	398	57
Nonpastoral	2,774	3,227	16	419	458	9

Note: Calculations assume "pre-decentralization" *woreda* boundaries
Source of data: SNNPR BOFED.

Table 4.4. Recurrent Expenditure Per Primary Student in SNNPR, 2001 and 2004 (n=104 *woredas*) (real Birr, 2004 prices)			
Type of *Woreda*	2001	2004	Percentage Change
Remote (more than 50 kilometers from a zonal capital)	114	137	20
Nonremote (less than 50 kilometers from a zonal capital)	129	150	16
Food insecure	120	140	16
Food secure	121	146	21
Pastoral	236	286	21
Nonpastoral	119	141	18

Note: Calculations assume "pre-decentralization" *woreda* boundaries.
Source of data: SNNPR BOFED and SNNPR Bureau of Education.

Table 4.5. Recurrent Expenditure Per Secondary Student in SNNPR, 2001 and 2004 (n=104 *woredas*) (real Birr, 2004 prices)			
Type of *Woreda*	2001	2004	Percentage Change
Remote (more than 50 kilometers from a zonal capital)	103	202	96
Nonremote (less than 50 kilometers from a zonal capital)	134	199	49
Food insecure	96	210	119
Food secure	168	175	4

Note: Calculations assume "pre-decentralization" *woreda* boundaries.
Source of data: SNNPR BOFED and SNNPR Bureau of Education.

After *Woreda*-Level Decentralization Began, Some Evidence of Lagging *Woredas* Partly Catching Up in Social Service Delivery

Gross primary education enrollment rates (GERs) have soared in both SNNPR and Oromiya within the three years since decentralization to *woreda*s began in 2002/03, continuing a nationwide trend that started several years earlier. *Woreda*-level data show an improvement in GERs over this three-year period of about 10 percent in SNNPR and 15 percent in the Oromiya subsample of *woreda*s (Tables 4.6 and 4.7). This rate of improvement is high even by international standards.

Over the same period, educational quality indicators largely declined, with the exception of repetition rates in SNNPR which fell from 11.9 percent to 10 percent (Tables 4.6 and 4.7). Repetition rates rose in Oromiya, as did pupil-teacher ratios and pupil-section ratios in both regions. This reflects the rapidly rising demand for primary schooling observed throughout Ethiopia, with supply often not being able to keep pace.

More interestingly, the coefficient of variation (Tables 4.6 and 4.7) in education outcomes was, in most cases, smaller in 2004 (after decentralization) compared to 2001 (before decen-

Table 4.6. Education Outcomes in SNNPR, 2001 and 2004 (n=123 *woredas*)

Item	Mean 2001	Mean 2004	Coefficient of Variation, 2001	Coefficient of Variation, 2004
Primary gross enrollment ratio	62.6%	72.9%	0.57	0.47
Proportion passing Grade 8 exams	71.3%	74.2%	0.23	0.19
Primary repetition rate	11.9%	10.0%	0.48	0.48
Primary pupil-teacher ratio	63.4	67.2	0.45	0.36
Primary pupil-section ratio	76.8	80.2	0.26	0.26
Primary teacher-section ratio	1.21	1.19	0.34	0.18

Note: The calculations assume "post-decentralization" boundaries and each locality covered by an urban administration—each urban district—is thus treated as a separate unit.
Source of data: SNNPR Bureau of Education.

Table 4.7. Primary Education Outcomes in Oromiya, 2001 and 2004 (n=69 *woredas*)

Item	Mean 2001	Mean 2004	Coefficient of Variation, 2001	Coefficient of Variation, 2004
Gross enrollment rate	53.6%	68.7%	0.27	0.22
Repetition rate	3.6%	4.9%	0.71	0.44
Pupil-teacher ratio	59.35	72.50	0.30	0.31
Pupil-section ratio	64.14	73.24	0.18	0.17
Teacher-section ratio	1.13	1.06	0.20	0.17

Note: The above figures were calculated for a subsample of 69 out of 197 *woredas* in Oromiya region (using "post-decentralization boundaries—see the introduction to this chapter for an explanation of this, and see also the footnote for the previous table"). The means are close to the overall regional means from official statistics.
Source: Oromiya Bureau of Education.

tralization). Unlike the standard deviation or variance, the coefficient of variation is comparable across distributions and is thus the appropriate variability measure to use here. The result indicates that education outcomes across *woredas* have become more equal, with some evidence of catching up by lagging *woredas*. This mirrors similar findings for spending measures, as reported above for both SNNPR (Table 4.1) and Oromiya (Table 4.2).

The "catch-up" trend for lagging *woredas* is, however, less evident in Oromiya compared to SNNPR. Indeed, in some cases the equalization of outcomes across *woredas* may be due more to a deterioration in *woredas* that are ahead, than to "catching up" by lagging *woredas*. This is especially true where there has been a sharp deterioration of indicators, as in the case of repetition rates and pupil-teacher ratios in Oromiya.

The above findings are confirmed by an analysis of educational outcomes by subgroupings of *woredas* for SNNPR. This exercise was not possible for Oromiya due to data limitations. The analysis for SNNPR shows that between 2001 and 2004—i.e., before and after decentralization—there has been significant "catch-up" by lagging *woredas* in several educational outcomes (Figures 4.3 to 4.5). These improvements mirror the changes in spending patterns analyzed above, which also disproportionately favored lagging *woredas* in SNNPR (Tables 4.3 to 4.5).

Pastoral *woredas* in SNNPR seem to have benefited most since the start of the *woreda*-level decentralization, perhaps because they started from a low base (Figures 4.4 to 4.6). These *woredas* enjoyed the greatest improvement in primary repetition rates and Grade 8 examination pass rates. Pastoral *woredas* still fall behind in overall enrollment and have a long way to go before they reach the 65 to 80 percent gross enrollment rate achieved by the rest of the region, but they have been improving more rapidly than other *woredas*. Again, this mirrors the finding above that the pastoral *woredas* benefited disproportionately in terms of increases in spending.

These findings are further confirmed by regression analysis (see Appendix C), which also shows that there has been equalization of outcomes at the school level within *woredas* in SNNPR. More specifically, since the start of decentralization lagging schools have been "catching up" in educational outcome indicators such as repetition rates and Grade 8 examination pass rates.

The figures show that remote and food-insecure *woredas* have been catching up in terms of gross enrollment ratios, but Grade 8 exam pass rates have not changed. These findings suggest that many other factors affect student performance, such as family socioeconomic status and other demand-side factors.

Teacher Redeployment Across *Woredas* and Within *Woredas*

One of the most important features of decentralization was the devolution of management of resources, including human resources, to the *woredas*, which are responsible for deploying

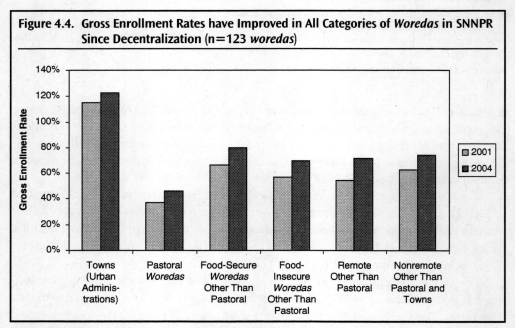

Figure 4.4. **Gross Enrollment Rates have Improved in All Categories of *Woredas* in SNNPR Since Decentralization (n=123 *woredas*)**

Note: Calculations assume "post-decentralization" boundaries.
Source of data: SNNPR Bureau of Education.

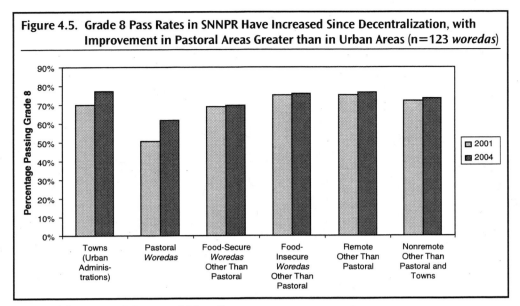

Figure 4.5. Grade 8 Pass Rates in SNNPR Have Increased Since Decentralization, with Improvement in Pastoral Areas Greater than in Urban Areas (n=123 *woredas*)

Source of data: SNNPR Bureau of Education.

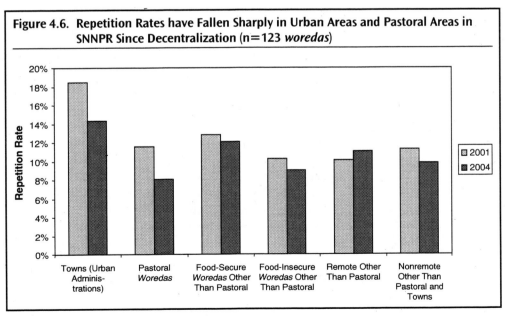

Figure 4.6. Repetition Rates have Fallen Sharply in Urban Areas and Pastoral Areas in SNNPR Since Decentralization (n=123 *woredas*)

Source of data: SNNPR Bureau of Education.

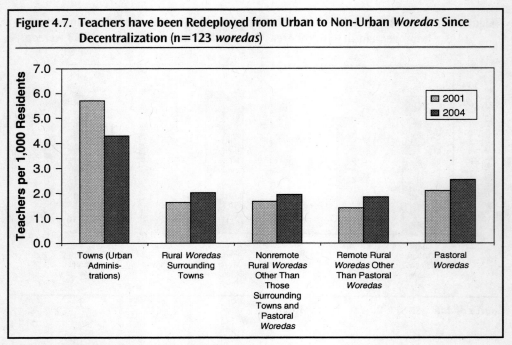

Figure 4.7. Teachers have been Redeployed from Urban to Non-Urban *Woredas* Since Decentralization (n=123 *woredas*)

Source of data: SNNPR Bureau of Education.

primary school teachers. Since decentralization, there has been a substantial redeployment of teachers in SNNPR, with the number of teachers in rural areas and nearby towns rising and the number of teachers in urban areas falling (Figure 4.7). A separate study (World Bank 2005a) observed that before decentralization, Ethiopia (except for Tigray) had a high degree of randomness in teacher deployment in government primary schools.

The redeployment of teachers from less-crowded schools in urban areas to overcrowded schools in rural areas increased pupil-teacher and reduced teacher-section ratios (ratio of number of teachers to number of sections) substantially in towns in SNNPR (Figure 4.8 to 4.9), with both ratios approaching the average levels in other *woreda* categories. The pupil-teacher ratio in towns (urban administrations) rose from 38 in 2001 to 54 in 2004, while the teacher-section ratio in towns fell from 2.0 in 2001 to 1.4 in 2004. This significant change in the teacher-section ratio in towns is a strong indicator of increased efficiency in teacher use since it indicates a rise in the average teaching load in towns to levels close to those in rural areas.[11] Despite the redeployment, pupil-teacher ratios in rural remote areas rose, because the increase in supply was insufficient to meet the large increase in demand. An analysis of the available data show clearly that these trends began in 2002 and not before, around the time that decentralization to the *woreda* level started.

11. In theory, a lower teacher-section ratio means one or more of the following: (i) a higher average teaching load; (ii) less average class time by students; (iii) increase in (or start in) rotation by some teachers between different classes, so that they handle two or more classes at the same time. Indications are that the first factor was the key one at play in the towns in SNNPR.

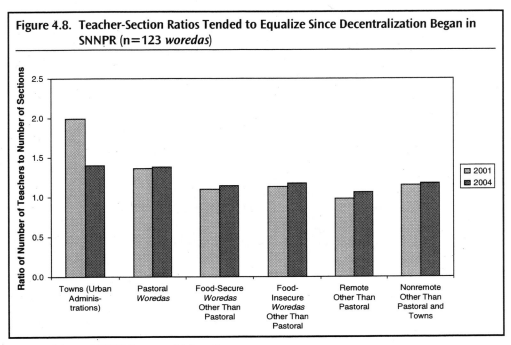

Figure 4.8.   Teacher-Section Ratios Tended to Equalize Since Decentralization Began in SNNPR (n=123 *woredas*)

Source of data: SNNPR Bureau of Education.

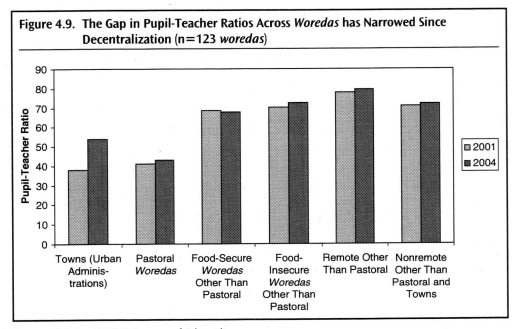

Figure 4.9.   The Gap in Pupil-Teacher Ratios Across *Woredas* has Narrowed Since Decentralization (n=123 *woredas*)

Source of data: SNNPR Bureau of Education.

It is unusual to see huge teacher reallocation happen in a short period of time, and with visible impact on pupil-teacher ratios across different areas. In SNNPR, several factors are likely to have contributed to this change:

- Firstly, starting at around the time of decentralization in 2002/03, the Regional Council with full support of the Regional Education Bureau started an explicit policy of reallocation of teachers from towns (with very low pupil-teacher ratios) to surrounding rural localities. An appropriate directive was issued, and zonal councils were also supportive.
- Secondly, the introduction of the "unit cost" block grant formula in SNNPR facilitated the equalization of pupil-teacher ratios. This is an explicit aim of the formula and is in line with the key overall objective of equalizing per student costs across *woredas* (see Box 3.1). Allocations to urban administrations were based on the same "unit cost" approach as allocations to rural *woredas,* and SNNPR differs in this sense from some other regions which allocate funding to urban administrations in a discretionary manner.[12]
- Thirdly, the "unit cost" approach had the effect of creating higher awareness and better planning by *woredas* and the region in the allocation of teachers, thereby facilitating the process of equalization of pupil-teacher ratios.
- Lastly, equalization of pupil-teacher ratios was achieved not just by reallocation of existing teachers away from towns (urban administrations), but also by appropriate placement of newly hired teachers in areas with high pupil-teacher ratios. The incentives given by the "unit cost" approach are especially important in this regard.

In Oromiya, this study finds no indication of teacher redeployment after decentralization. In fact Table 4.7 shows that the coefficient of variation of the distribution of *woreda* pupil-teacher ratios actually increased slightly after decentralization to the *woredas* began. Figure 4.10 shows that pupil-teacher ratios (PTRs) rose substantially in both high-PTR *woredas* and in low-PTR *woredas* between 2001 and 2004.

This finding from the Oromiya data illustrates that the introduction of the simple "three-parameter" block grant formula may not be sufficient to improve allocation of inputs such as teachers across *woredas*. On the other hand, SNNPR managed to substantially improve the efficiency of teacher allocation through the introduction of a block grant formula (using the unit cost approach) more suited for the purpose, and which was facilitated by an explicit sector policy on teacher reallocation supported at the highest levels in the region.

The "three-parameter" approach is especially unsuitable for equalizing pupil-teacher ratios given that the enrollment rate is not an explicit factor in the formula—higher enrollments do not mean higher block grant allocations.

Redeployment of teachers took place not only between *woredas* but also within *woredas* in SNNPR. As a result, differences in pupil-teacher ratios across schools within *woredas* narrowed (Figure 4.11). The pupil-teacher ratio (PTR) of schools below the median PTR within

---

12. A caveat here, as mentioned in Chapter 3, is that all urban administrations in SNNPR got allocations from a common pool, and all rural *woredas* also got allocations from a common pool—but these two pools were different. In making budget allocations, the region would decide independently how much funding to allocate to each of these pools. Regardless, for many "cost drivers" (see Box 3.1) such as the average pupil-teacher ratio, the aim was still to equalize them across and between rural *woredas* and towns (urban administrations).

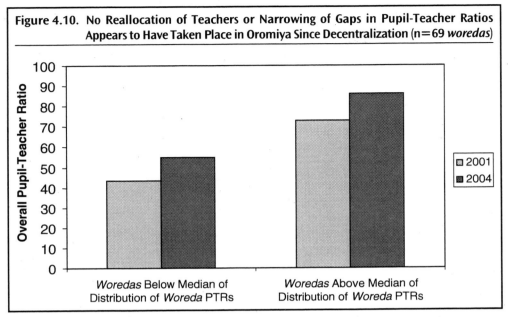

Figure 4.10. No Reallocation of Teachers or Narrowing of Gaps in Pupil-Teacher Ratios Appears to Have Taken Place in Oromiya Since Decentralization (n=69 *woredas*)

Source of data: Oromiya Bureau of Education.

each *woreda* rose from 58 to 64 since the start of decentralization, while that of schools above the median within each *woreda* fell, from 107 to 78. The available data show that this "narrowing" trend of within-*woreda* PTRs was not observed before decentralization; between 2000 and 2001, there was a rise in the PTR of schools below the median within-district PTR (from 56 to 58), as well as of schools above the median within-district PTR (from 104 to 107).

These findings are confirmed by the regression analysis presented in Appendix C. In all the regressions, the coefficient of the main independent variable of interest—the original 2001 value of the relevant educational indicator—is negative and statistically significant, in both the school-level and the *woreda*-level regressions. The regression results with the school pupil-teacher ratio as the dependent variable was based on analyses of 2,244 schools in the 123 *woreda*s in the region. They show that the differences in pupil-section ratios narrowed— that is, teachers were redeployed from schools with higher pupil-teacher ratio to schools with lower pupil-teacher ratios in order to reduce the imbalance in teacher allocation.

What this implies is that while the overall number of teachers may not have increased enough to accommodate the rapid growth in enrollment, the redeployment of teachers from less crowded schools to more crowded schools in SNNPR has likely improved the efficiency of the teaching force. This may be one factor contributing to the decline in repetition rates observed in most *woreda*s in the region.

Regression Analysis: Linking Expenditures with Outcomes

Summarizing the evidence presented so far in this chapter, with decentralization to *woreda*s in 2002/03, the gap in education outcomes between the lagging *woreda*s and the better-off

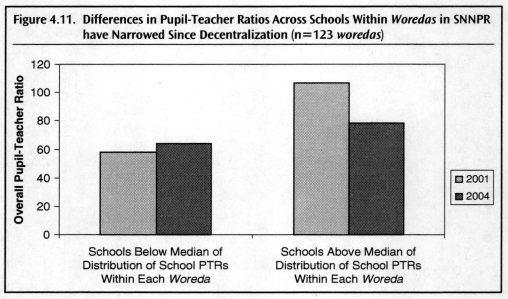

Figure 4.11. Differences in Pupil-Teacher Ratios Across Schools Within *Woredas* in SNNPR have Narrowed Since Decentralization (n=123 *woredas*)

Source of data: SNNPR Bureau of Education.

*woreda*s in SNNPR tended to narrow. There has been substantial equalization of pupil-teacher ratios across *woreda*s, achieved partly by extensive teacher reallocation from urban to rural areas. At the same time, the differences in per capita and per student education spending across *woreda*s have been narrowing, likely attributable mainly to the introduction of a formula-driven approach to determining block grant allocations.

The picture in Oromiya is somewhat different. There has also been substantial equalization of per capita and per student education spending across *woreda*s but this has not been accompanied by an actual improvement of allocation across *woreda*s of the main educational budgetary input—the teachers. Furthermore, there is evidence of "catching up" of lagging *woreda*s in gross enrollment rates but not in other indicators such as repetition rates.

The analysis in this section focuses on the evidence presented for SNNPR. Is there a clear relationship between spending and outcomes? What could explain the narrowing of per capita spending and educational outcomes across *woreda*s?

To explore this question, *woreda*-level regressions analyzing the effects of expenditure on education and health outcomes, controlling for variables related to infrastructure, level of development, population size, and location, were conducted. In addition, similar regressions were conducted with measures of teacher quantity—such as the pupil-teacher ratio and the number of teachers per 1,000 population—as right-hand side variables, to directly examine the impact of these variables on educational outcomes.

The results, presented in Appendix D, show that after controlling for other factors, increases in the levels of expenditure on education had a strong effect on increases in enrollment rates and in Grade 8 pass rates. A strong positive relationship is observed between changes in the level of teacher inputs and changes in enrollment rates as well as in Grade 8 pass rates. In an earlier study (World Bank 2005a), teacher inputs in Ethiopia were found to a strong impact on Grade 8 pass rates at the level of the individual student. That study did not find any relationship between *woreda*-level spending and Grade 8 pass rates—although it should be noted it was based on cross section data, compared to the present study which uses longitudinal data.

Primary gross enrollment rates rose with education expenditure, as did Grade 8 pass rates. Grade 8 pass rates also improved with per student primary expenditure. Primary gross enroll-ment rates rose with the number of teachers per 1,000 population while Grade 8 pass rates were found to rise as the pupil-teacher ratio declined. The results related to Grade 8 pass rates were obtained with samples restricted to poorly performing *woreda*s—those with especially low Grade 8 pass rates to begin with (see Appendix D for more details).

The regression results add weight to the hypothesis that there is a relationship between the observed "catching up" of lagging *woreda*s in educational outcomes on the one hand, and the equalization of spending measures as well as of pupil-teacher ratios on the other. The latter is likely attributable in large part to the introduction of formula-driven block grant allocations since the start of decentralization, especially the use of the "unit cost" approach. In turn, one can conclude that there is evidence that decentralization in SNNPR influenced the improvements observed with the lagging *woreda*s.

The regression analysis also confirms many of the earlier results from the descrip-tive analysis on the relative changes in education outcomes and in spending measures for specific groups of *woreda*s. For example, the regressions show that increases in gross enrollment rates are positively related to the distance of a *woreda* from the zonal capital, mirroring the earlier finding of especially large increases in enrollment rates in remote *woreda*s since decentralization started (see Figure 4.4). The changes in education expen-diture measures in remote *woreda*s (see Tables 4.3 to 4.5) add weight to the hypothesis that there is a relationship between the large increases in spending and the large rises in enrollment rates in remote *woreda*s.

The analysis in this chapter recognizes a number of limitations. Many other factors that cannot be measured have important effects on the outcomes of interest. Education outcomes are affected by sector policies such as reallocation of teachers, as well as by the contributions of communities and leadership in the region and the *woreda*. Communi-ties have been contributing material, funding, and support to schools through the con-struction and management of schools through PTAs. Likewise, the effects of household socio-economic factors cannot be easily accounted for in an analysis that uses the *woreda* as the unit of investigation.

Decentralization's High Potential to Improve Service Delivery

Based on the available evidence, decentralization has already contributed to positive changes in service delivery in education and health in SNNPR. Total enrollment rates and Grade 8 pass rates in poorly performing *woreda*s rose with education expenditure growth, and both also rose with increases in teacher inputs. Repetition rates in poorly performing *woreda*s fell with increases in teacher inputs. The data show that since decentralization started, there has been an equalization of spending measures and pupil-teacher ratios across *woreda*s on the one hand, and an equalization of educational outcomes—with "catching up" of lagging *woreda*s—on the other. The regression results imply that there is a relationship between these two.

These results imply also that there is a discernible level effect of increasing expenditure on improving enrollment. Many *woredas* increased their education budgets, which appears to have increased enrollment. As seen in Chapter 5, the results were achieved in an environment with constraints in both capacity and monitoring. This indicates that, even with improving capacity, better outcomes can be achieved.

The implementation of decentralization with formula-driven block grant allocations in SNNPR has clearly shifted the bias in expenditures toward the lagging and disadvantaged *woredas*. Lagging food-insecure, pastoral, and remote *woredas* have begun to catch up in terms of outcomes and have benefited disproportionately in terms of per capita spending.

One possible explanation for the equalizing effects of decentralization observed in SNNPR is the use of the unit cost approach to determine how to allocate block grants from regions across *woredas*. In contrast to the three-parameter formula used in most other regions, the unit cost approach helped to reduce the gap in per student teacher allocations and pupil-teacher ratios across *woredas*. It also provides incentives for increasing efficiency in the deployment of teachers. Because teachers account for a large proportion of the recurrent education spending of *woredas*, in an environment of limited budgets, sustainable improvements in service delivery cannot occur without improving the deployment of teachers from less crowded classrooms to more crowded classrooms.

Equally important for the teacher reallocations in SNNPR was the implementation of a specific sector policy favoring teacher reallocation from towns (urban administrations) to rural *woredas*. This policy emanated from the highest levels—the Regional Council—and had the full support of the Regional Educational Bureau as well as the zonal councils.

In Oromiya, there has been equalization of per capita and per student education spending across *woredas*, but no equalization of pupil-teacher ratios nor any real teacher reallocation. The latter is likely attributable to: (i) the use of the three-parameter block grant formula that does not purposely target the equalization of pupil-teacher ratios; as well as (ii) the lack of a specific policy favoring teacher reallocation.

Gross enrollment rates have risen and their distribution has become more equal across *woredas*. However, repetition rates in Oromiya have also risen, and this appears to have occurred disproportionately in *woredas* with low repetition rates to begin with. Thus the picture in terms of improvement of educational outcomes is mixed, just as the picture in terms of educational inputs—such as teachers and spending measures—is mixed. Certainly, the path taken by SNNPR is clearly a more favorable one.

It could be argued that the equalization across districts of spending and outcomes, observed in SNNPR and to a more limited extent in Oromiya, is largely attributable to a more equal distribution of resources across *woredas*, and could have occurred without an increase in accountability and autonomy at the local level. Indeed, some argue that decentralization to the district level is still very new, and that—following the experience of other countries—it would take time for significant increases to be seen in true local-level accountability/autonomy (see Box 3.3). Even if local-level accountability and autonomy are still limited, however, decentralization has clearly been very beneficial in obliging the use of a formula-based approach to distributing resources across *woredas*. This appears to have resulted in measurable benefits, especially in SNNPR. In theory, a formula-based approach to resource allocation across *woredas* could have been possible even without district-level decentralization. Yet, decentralization made this approach feasible in practice.

It should also be pointed out that the observed narrowing of school pupil-teacher ratios within *woreda*s, which began after district-level decentralization in SNNPR, cannot be explained by the introduction of a formula-based approach to resource allocation across *woreda*s. Here, there is a stronger rationale for an explanation pointing to increased autonomy and accountability at the local level, due to decentralization.

Decentralization appears to have already improved service delivery in poorer locations, at least in SNNPR. These changes are occurring even where capacity has not reached anywhere near the *woreda*s' potential. With further improvement in *woreda* capacity, and with the use of appropriate formula for block grant allocations as well as appropriate sector policies, decentralization may contribute significantly to achieving the targets for improving health and education in Ethiopia.

CHAPTER 5

Making Decentralization Work

Overcoming Constraints in Decentralized Service Delivery

Decentralization has shown the potential for facilitating the delivery of basic social services through modest increases in the control of resources, increased spending for social services, and service delivery being more responsive and more flexible. The analysis in the previous chapter has shown that the beneficial effects can be fully realized with adequate levels of fiscal transfers to *woreda*s, and with the use of appropriate methods of distributing these resources across *woreda*s. In addition, optimal results can be realized if sector policies are aligned with the goals of decentralization as amply demonstrated in SNNPR.

Critical Constraints

Despite these improvements, however, critical constraints continue to stymie the efficient and effective delivery of services. Failure to address these constraints could negate the achievements made to date. This chapter identifies some of these constraints and proposes options for overcoming them.

Inadequate Resources at the Woreda *Level*

Lower tiers of government in Ethiopia have substantial responsibility for meeting targets in education, health, and water and sanitation. But financing from block grants has not been sufficient to allow them to provide these basic services. In 2004/05 about 26 percent of the federal budget was transferred to the regions as unconditional grants (35 percent when special purpose grants are included) (Figure 5.1). These transfers provided

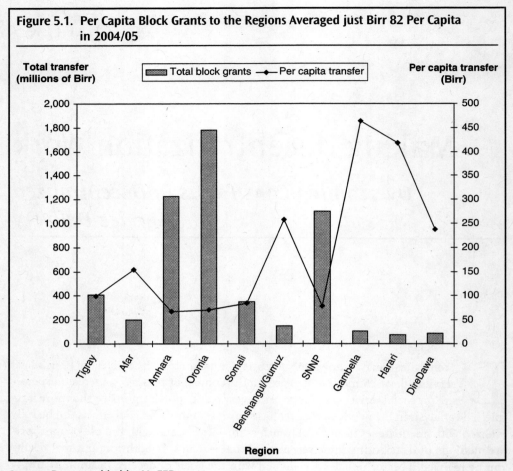

Figure 5.1. Per Capita Block Grants to the Regions Averaged just Birr 82 Per Capita in 2004/05

Source: Data provided by MoFED.

the average region with just 82 Birr per capita to undertake all the development activities within its mandate. Adding regions' own resources to the pool increases spending to just 108 Birr per capita.

The constraints imposed by inadequate financing are even tighter at the *woreda* level (Figure 5.2). In the Four Main Decentralizing Regions, the regions transfer between 51 percent (Oromiya) and 78 percent (SNNP) of the unconditional block grants they receive from the federal government. The average *woreda* in SNNPR and Oromiya allocates 45 percent of its recurrent resources to education, 90 percent of which goes to salaries (Dom 2004).

During the initial period of decentralization to the *woreda*s, 34 of 123 *woreda*s in SSNPR lacked adequate budgets. According to *woreda*-level officials, this lack of funds made it difficult for them to expand or improve the quality of services. *Woreda*s financial resources have been improving, as transfers from regions have increased. Moreover, not all *woreda*s face the same budget predicament. Nevertheless, the lack of adequate budgets remains a serious constraint.

Although the overall national expenditure envelop has increased substantially over the past seven to eight years, grants from the federal government to subnational governments

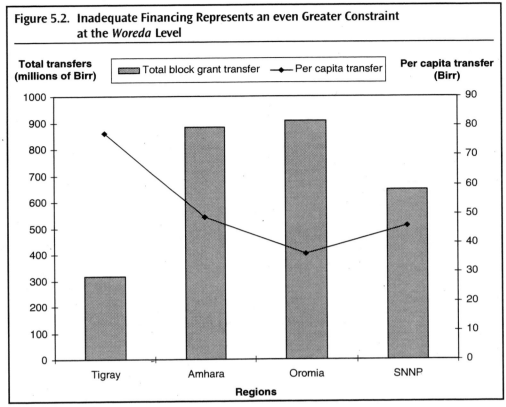

Figure 5.2. Inadequate Financing Represents an even Greater Constraint at the *Woreda* Level

Note: Data are for 2004/05.
Source: Data Provided by MoFED.

through block grant transfers have not risen as rapidly, although this pattern is now changing (see below). As a proportion of federal revenues, block grant transfers to regions fell, from about 73 percent in 2000/01 to about 46 percent in 2004/05 (Table 5.1).[13] This appears to indicate a need for much larger block grant transfers, to enable subnational governments to fulfill their commitments to the delivery of basic services at the lower levels in the face of rapidly increasing demands. However, the figures do not take into account the sharp increase in Federal funding for Special Purpose Grants which appear only on the Federal budget but are executed at the regional level (see Figure 5.4). It should also be noted that a significant portion of the increase in Federal spending has gone towards basic services; for example, the new rural electrification program took up about 6 percent of total Federal revenue (including grants) in 2005/06.

In any case, the Federal government has made commitments to increase block grant transfers to the regions substantially over the next few years, with support from the multi-

---

13. Debt repayments, interest payments, external assistance and defense spending were subtracted from total Federal revenue (including grants) before making these percentage calculations (see Table 5.1).

donor Protecting Basic Services operation which began in June 2006. This trend has already begun. Total block grant transfers to the regions in 2006/07 were 9.4 billion Birr, as compared to 5.5 billion Birr in 2004/05. According to the latest draft MEFF, block grant transfers will rise by 4 billion Birr a year for the next three years, reaching 21.56 billion Birr in 2009/10. If these commitments are fulfilled, the trend shown in Table 5.1 where the vertical allocation of resources has been shifting against the regions would be firmly reversed.

Table 5.1. Block Grant Transfers as a Proportion of Federal Revenues, 1996/97–2005/06 (millions of Birr)

	1997/98	2000/01	2001/02	2002/03	2003/04	2004/05	2005/06
Federal Revenues Including Grants	7,649	11,132	9,845	12,808	14,834	16,576	18,865
Federal Revenues net of Interest Payments, Debt Repayments, External Assistance and Defense (A)	4,459	4,874	5,172	6,358	10,603	11,924	14,216
Block Grant Transfers (B)	3,233	3,548	3,996	4,523	5,021	5,498	7,071
B as percentage of A	73%	73%	77%	71%	47%	46%	50%

Note: All figures reflect actual revenues and expenditures.
Source: Data provided by MoFED.

Difficulty in Planning Due to Inadequate Information

In principle, budget planning involves elements of a "bottom-up" participatory approach, in which communities and *woreda* offices of education, health, and water and sanitation set priorities and goals, which are then approved by the *woreda* council before submission to the regional government. In practice, most regions do not know the size of their grant before the end of the third quarter or the beginning of the fourth quarter. As a result, most the planning is mechanical and often turns into a wish list exercise. The poor information base and uncertainty regarding the budget envelop also undermines the credibility of long-term planning, even though most frontline service providers do produce three-year development plans, and it undermines budgeting for capital expenditures. If basic services in education, health, and water and sanitation are to improve, the resources available to *woreda*s must be adequate and predictable (World Bank 2004a).

Need to Improve Clarity in Expenditure Assignments and Responsibilities

The expenditure assignments between levels of government have not yet been fully defined, although much progress has been made in this regard. It is not realistic to expect all issues of expenditure assignment and the corresponding responsibilities to have been sorted out less than five years after the start of decentralization to the *woreda* level. However, expenditure assignments must be clearer and serve as the basis for the allocation of resources across tiers of government.

For accountability mechanisms to be effective and service delivery to improve, delegation of responsibilities must be matched by adequate finances especially at the local government level, and expenditure assignments of the different levels of government need to be fully and clearly defined. This does not yet happen to a sufficient degree in Ethiopia. Expenditure assignments are in many ways the starting point for fiscal frameworks, because they represent the functional parameters for financial flows. Lack of clear assignments can lead to duplicated effort and lack of coordination. It also makes it difficult to assign budgets in order to meet functional objectives.

In the regions that have instituted *woreda*-level decentralization, practices regarding assigning responsibilities to various levels of government have been evolving. The regions, zones, and *woreda*s are clear about the broad areas of recurrent expenditure managed by each level of government in education and health.

Responsibilities in other areas are less clear. In some regions, for example, regional, zonal and local authorities are all responsible for "prevention and control of HIV/AIDS", with no indication of exactly what is expected of them, how they are supposed to complement each other, or how much each level is supposed to contribute. Not only are these distinctions weak or absent, there is no clear link to fiscal capacity and responsibility. Functional and fiscal assignments need to be clearly tied and assignments costed as accurately as possible in order to eliminate any disjuncture between functional accountability and fiscal arrangements.

Within each of the broadly assigned areas of responsibility, the exact roles of each level of government and institution need to be made clearer (Box 5.1). While *woreda*s' functional assignments indicate that they are responsible for recruitment and retrenchment, for example, in practice the zones have often overruled their decisions about retrenchment (Heymans and Mussa 2004), although there are indications that this may be changing at least in some regions.

Substantial progress is being made, however, in defining expenditure assignments of different levels of government, especially in the four larger regions which began decentralization first (Amhara, Oromiya, SNNPR and Tigray). These regions revised their constitutions in 2001; these constitutions are the basis for decentralization of power to *woreda*s. The next step would be for each region to adopt a legal framework clearly spelling out expenditure assignments and the division of responsibilities between different levels of government.

To ensure that this would happen and as a guide to the regions, a draft prototype legal framework was developed in March 2006, as a model on which regional legal frameworks were supposed to be based. Among other things, the draft framework provided details and regulations on the structure and composition of different tiers of administration; assignments at the regional, *woreda* and kebele level for different service delivery functions; conduct of official meetings; powers and functions of different actors; financial provisions; inter governmental relationships; human resource and management issues; and miscellaneous provisions.

Following this, each of the regions is now taking measures to finalize its legal framework for decentralization to *woreda*s. Tigray has made significant progress in providing such a framework (see Box 5.1). Amhara has produced a draft regulation laying out a legal framework, which has been submitted to the regional administration for further comments and approval. In SNNP, a workshop on this legal framework has been conducted by the Bureau of Capacity Building; selected *woreda* staff were invited to give feedback and comments. In Oromiya, work is under way on this legal framework, and a consultant has been recruited for this purpose. Furthermore, all of the four larger regions have adopted municipal proclamations which lay out responsibilities and assignments of municipalities.

Even without an appropriate legal framework for decentralization to *woreda*s, regions usually have written functional assignments for different sectors, but these are not always operational. Hiring of certain types of personnel, for instance, is the responsibility of the *woreda*s, but in some instances zones hire staff when the *woreda*s cannot find candidates in their area. In principle, firing and transferring staff are the responsibilities of the *woreda*s, but their decisions are sometimes overruled by the regional bureaus or zones, without consultation. The region sometimes arbitrarily makes decisions about transferring health workers and teachers who serve in rural *woreda*s, which creates tension between the *woreda*s and the region. According to some *woreda* officials, the unplanned transfer of frontline workers to the *woreda* has caused budget deficits and made it impossible for the *woreda* to pay salaries. But all of this can be expected to improve soon, as long as regions finalize the establishment of the legal frameworks for decentralization to *woreda*s, and then enforce these frameworks.

Box 5.1. Improving the Legal Framework for Decentralization in Tigray

The Tigray region has made significant progress in providing a legal framework for decentralization. In early 2006 the Regional Council proclaimed two acts, "Strengthening Decentralization" and "Organization and Tasks and Responsibilities of *Woreda* Executive Bodies". These acts go a long way toward clarifying the regional legal and policy framework for decentralization. They formalize existing practice, legally establishing the *woreda* block grant mechanism and linking *woreda* functional assignments to resources. They provide further clarity on other points, such as *woreda* functional assignments; *woreda* participatory planning and its link with the regional strategic planning policies; and regional support to and oversight of *woreda*s. They also break new ground in a number of important dimensions, such as providing a framework for assigning revenues to *woreda*s and allowing for flexibility in *woreda*s' administrative structures and staffing policies.

Particularly difficult is the issue of who is responsible for the capital budget. Regions increasingly pass on responsibility for capital investment to the *woreda*s. In FY 2004/2005, for instance, about 49 percent of education capital investment by the regions was budgeted at the *woreda* level (Dom 2004). Giving *woreda*s some responsibility for planning and financing development makes sense, but in practice they often control little of the capital budget. Reluctance to devolve more control to the *woreda*s is rooted in several tensions in the system. One is the thorny issue of how best to finance capital spending. Should it come from the block grant? Should there be a special purpose grant for capital spending? If *woreda*s are required to finance capital expenditures from the block grant, will there be any assurance that funds will not be diverted to more pressing recurrent expenditure needs, given the unconditional nature of the block grant? Another difficult issue is the fear by federal and regional governments that planning and managing complex capital investments may be beyond the capacity of many *woredas*. Not surprisingly these tensions remain unresolved and have tended to favor the creation of special purpose grants, even though the signals in the government's financial reporting system (most directly from the execution of capital budgets) seem to suggest that caution is needed in providing special purpose grants.

A very visible example of the ambiguity in responsibility for capital investment management is secondary education (Dom 2004). *Woredas* are responsible for the first cycle of secondary education (Grades 9–10). While this makes sense in large and populated *woredas*, where enrollment potential is high, in smaller *woredas* demand may be insufficient. Allowing *woredas* to make their own decisions about secondary education may lead to the proliferation of small and costly schools.

Despite this problem, all regions have encouraged *woredas* to increase their capital expenditures. But pressure on *woredas* to meet their recurrent expenditure obligations has limited their scope for capital investments. The *woredas* are also reluctant to commit funds to capital expenses early on, because they are legally prohibited from changing such allocations back to the recurrent side of the budget. The current system risks perpetuating this trend in that the assumption is that most capital investment falls within the ambit of federal and regional responsibilities. Furthermore, many *woredas* have been limited by the lack of adequate staff to deal with the challenge of capital budgeting and capital investment implementation.

A more complex capital budget allocation issue is how externally funded programs are treated in the envelop of resources allocated by block grants to *woredas*. At the Federal level, the full amount expected to be spent by each region from external project-specific (and on-budget) funding is subtracted or "offset" from the region's block grant allocation. Thus, each additional Birr that a region gets in project-specific funding results in a one Birr reduction in its block grant allocation, that is, there is 100 percent offsetting. At the regional level, there is variation in the extent of "offsetting" of project-specific funding from block grant allocations to *woredas*. In some cases, there is full (100 percent) offsetting, while in other cases there is partial or no offsetting from *woreda* block grant allocations. Offsetting can be problematic because it results, in effect, in high fungibility of external aid; providing project-specific funding becomes almost like providing untied funding. In addition, offsetting reduces the incentive for regions or *woredas* to accept external project-specific funding; given the choice between project-specific funding and an equivalent amount of untied block grant funding, many regions/*woredas* would accept the latter. This is because project-specific funding flows are often unpredictable, and the projects can often impose a significant bureaucratic burden.

Declining Share of Spending on Capital Expenditures by Subnational Governments

As decentralization to *woredas* went into full swing in 2002/3 in the four largest regions, there was a strong belief that many *woredas* were not investing much in capital and that the newly found autonomy would lead local governments to spend on recurrent expenditures, in particular salaries. In fact, capital spending by subnational governments

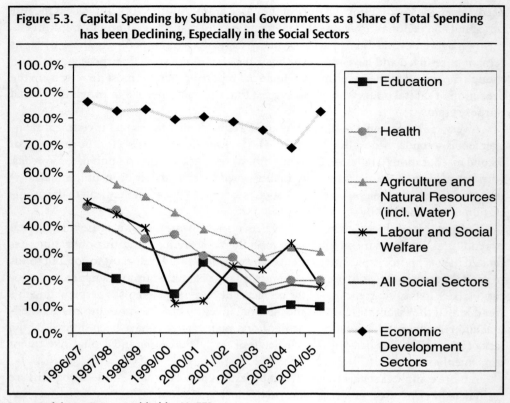

Figure 5.3. Capital Spending by Subnational Governments as a Share of Total Spending has been Declining, Especially in the Social Sectors

Source of data: Data provided by MoFED.

(regional bureaus, zones and *woreda*s) as a share of total spending has been declining steadily over the past several years, a trend that started before decentralization to the *woreda*s began (Figure 5.3). The declining shares are particularly evident in the social sectors, including education and health.

The evidence suggests that low capital spending by *woreda*s may often be due more to a lack of resources than a suboptimal desire to spend on capital relative to recurrent spending. Regional guidelines as to appropriate capital budget shares for the *woreda*s may be useful, but they are unlikely to work unless adequate resources are transferred. Concerned about suboptimal capital spending for budget items handled by the *woreda*s, in 2004 the Oromiya regional government issued a guideline that *woreda*s should spend 8–10 percent of their budgets on capital items. Despite this, in 2005/06 just 7 percent of total *woreda*s budgets in Oromiya were allocated to capital items. Yet in the same year, *woreda*s allocated 16 percent of their total budgets to capital items in Tigray. This higher share of capital spending in Tigray was probably facilitated in turn by the much higher per capita block grant allocation to *woreda*s in Tigray than in Oromiya. As a result of the latter, 2005/06, the per capita total budget (recurrent plus capital) of *woreda*s in Tigray was 113 Birr, as opposed to 63 Birr in Oromiya.

Overall, the capital share of total subnational spending has been falling for several years before 2002/03, but has remained roughly constant since then. Similarly, real per capita capital subnational spending has also remained more or less constant since 2002/03. For the social sectors, the capital share of total subnational government spending (excluding Addis Ababa) has remained at about 17 percent since 2002/03 (Figure 5.3). For the eco-nomic development sectors, the capital share rose from 75.3 percent in 2002/03 to 82.3 per-cent in 2004/05 before falling to 76.5 percent in 2005/06.

Despite a fall until 2002/03 and then stagnation in real per capita capital spending by subnational governments, there appears to have been acceleration in physical investment in capital stock related to primary service delivery over the same period. In the education sector, between 2002/03 and 2004/05, the number of new primary schools created per 10 million people was 5.9, up from 4.2 in the two years preceding decentralization to the *woreda* level (Figure 5.4). More new secondary schools and new health posts were created per 1 million people between 2002/03 and 2004/05 than between 1999/00 and 2001/02.

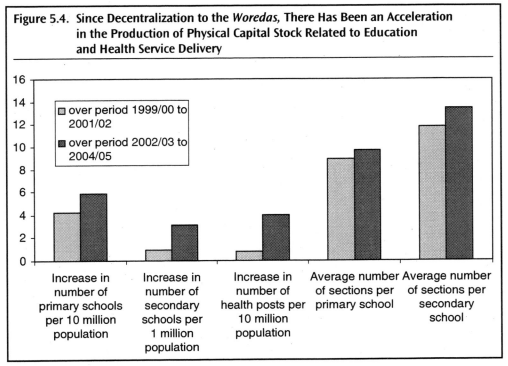

Figure 5.4. Since Decentralization to the *Woredas,* There Has Been an Acceleration in the Production of Physical Capital Stock Related to Education and Health Service Delivery

Source: Official Data from Ministries of Education and Health.

Furthermore, there is some evidence that the productivity of these capital investments has risen since decentralization. One measure of the productivity of the capital stock in the education sector is the average number of sections per school. This figure rose from 9.2 in 1999/2000–2001/02 to 10.3 in 2002/03–2004/05. One explanation for the rise is the increase in the number of double-shift schools during the period. There is one caveat to note, how-ever. Many of the new schools and health posts have been built by communities with limited government assistance, and there is some concern that some of these may be of substandard quality.

In sum, declines in capital spending in the education or health sector—in real per capita terms or as a share of total spending—is not necessarily an indication of inadequate capital spending. Nor does it imply a misalignment between capital and recurrent spending.

The acceleration in the production of new schools and health posts is likely to be a result of various factors, including shifts to low-cost construction and substantial increases in community contributions. The Ministry of Education has estimated annual community contributions in the sector to be about Birr 11 per capita in 2005/06.

One should also note that the above analysis is based on data on spending that occurs through subnational government budgets. It does not capture the large amount of off-budget capital spending on local service delivery. This includes not just the community contributions that have just been referred to, but also the increasing amount of local spending undertaken by NGOs, especially in the health sector.

One problem is that there is evidence that many *woreda*s have limited capacity to execute capital spending, especially where donor funds are involved. Building capacity at the *woreda* level to execute capital investment is critical.

Need for Mechanisms to Address the Differences in Revenue Generating Capacity of Woredas

The *woreda* budget consists of transfers from the region and own revenues. The current practice is to fix a target revenue collection for each *woreda* and use that as a basis for determining the level of block grant transfers to the *woreda*. More specifically, a predetermined formula is used to determine the block grant allocation to each *woreda*. From this allocation, the targeted revenue collection for that *woreda* is subtracted to derive the transfer from the region to that *woreda*. This practice has been challenged by *woreda*s, on the grounds that the targets are often not feasible or that the *woreda*s may not be able to meet the targets in some circumstances. A recent review found that the targets were negotiated in Oromiya, but SNNPR's policy was to generally avoid topping up the transfer element of the block grant in favor of defaulting *woreda*s. Instead, the region generally lent funds needed to make up for shortfalls. This practice negatively affected service delivery in Wonego *woreda* in SNNPR, where the non-salary component of the education recurrent budget was cut by 50 percent in 2003/04, hampering the delivery of primary school materials (Dom 2004). In another *woreda*, Alaba, there were shortfalls in teacher salaries, training, textbooks, some office supplies, and supervision budgets.

The regional governments do not yet have clear mechanisms for sharing revenues with the *woreda*s. *Woreda*s collect revenue on behalf of the regions, and the collected revenue is part of each *woreda*'s block grant. In Tigray an act on revenue-sharing mechanisms between the region and the *woreda*s has been approved by the regional council and has been officially issued in Negaret Gazeta as a proclamation. Other regions have attempted to draft acts on revenue-sharing mechanisms, but these drafts have not yet become official documents.

Revenue sources are broadly categorized as direct taxes, indirect taxes, and non-tax revenues (more detailed breakdowns could not be obtained). Direct taxes include personal income taxes, rental income taxes, and business income taxes; indirect taxes include taxes on works contracts, stamp duties, income from work permits, court fees, and business registration fees. Direct taxes are the major source of revenue, followed by non-tax revenues.

*Woreda*s obtain their revenue from land, agricultural, business, and income taxes, as well as from license fees and fines for minor crimes. City governments have similar sources of revenue, but they collect revenue from about 20 taxes, including property taxes, market transaction taxes, and charges on services rendered, such as water provision. The revenue collected by municipalities is used to carry out municipal functions; in the case of short-falls, they do not receive support from the region. The revenue collected is fully managed by the municipalities, which do not transfer resources to the treasury.

No revenue-sharing mechanism is in place in SNNPR, but a study is underway on rev-enue potential and capacity that is expected to lead to revenue-sharing legislation for the region. The *woreda* administrations vary greatly in institutional and fiscal capacity, ranging from those with substantial own-revenue bases (mostly in peri-urban areas such as Awassa Zuria) to ones without much of a fiscal base and very low capacity (such as Boritcha, a recently created *woreda* in a rural area that is highly food-insecure). In 2002/03, Awassa Zuria received 56 percent of its budget from the regional government and raised 44 percent of its budget through local revenue. In contrast, Boritcha's own-revenue contribution was 10 percent; 90 percent of its budget came from the regional block grant.

In 2004, Oromiya attempted to introduce a revenue-sharing mechanism between the regional government and *woreda* administrations. It identified revenue as a key issue, acknowledging that some local areas make considerable contributions not only to local rev-enue but also to the regional treasury funds. For example, in Aweday, in eastern Hararghe, the center of Ethiopia's tchat (a tobacco-like cash crop) industry, substantial collections could increase overall regional revenues.

The region seems to have made some progress in allowing local structures to retain at least part of their surpluses (the amount of own revenue collected in excess of the expected revenue collection, if any), but this approach has not been fully consolidated and surpluses are still largely offset against the block grant. The region does recognize that local use of sur-pluses without being offset by the block grant can become a strong incentive for local rev-enue generation. The prospects for local governments improving their revenue performance in the short term are constrained by the limited capacity of local government officials to effectively administer a revenue system; the prevalence of weak administration procedures; poor record keeping, and inefficient and irregular updating of tax rolls; inefficient collec-tion procedures; and inadequate information about tax bases.

Even where local governments can keep all or most of their own revenue surpluses, the treatment of own revenues in most regions is problematic. In effect, if a *woreda* takes steps to improve its own revenue collection, it is raising expectations of its own revenue collection in future years, thereby reducing its block grant transfer from the region in future years. In this respect, the "fiscal equalization" approach under consideration for Federal block grant transfers to the regions is superior since *woreda*s would, in effect, be allowed to "keep" all their own revenues; the approach would not reduce *woreda*s' incen-tive to collect own revenues. (See Appendix B for more on this; Chapter 3 describes briefly the "fiscal equalization" approach.)

Need to Improve Monitoring and Enforcement

Except for urban municipalities, which are expected to be self-financing, most *woreda*s finance the services for which they are responsible through the unconditional block grant. The unconditional nature of the grant has the desirable feature of granting the *woreda*s significant discretion to pursue local priorities in budget allocation. Until now, the federal and regional governments relied on informal understandings and consensus on national goals to guide spending priorities. However, within this flexibility enjoyed by local governments, in most regions there is no institutionalized system to encourage good performance.

Currently, SNNPR is the only region that has initiated a process designed to promote good performance; it has introduced "performance agreements" (see Box 3.2). The region is also planning to introduce a system that will require each *woreda* administration to development a three-year sectoral public expenditure program (PEP), which would link consolidated (regional and *woreda*) sector financial requirements to agreed upon/expected sector performance. The PEPs would be embedded within a regional Medium-Term Expenditure and Financial Framework, and the first year of the PEP would be the basis for preparation of the following year's annual fiscal plan and budget. This approach would provide *woreda*s with firmer "pre-budget ceilings" for the first step of the *woreda* budgeting cycle.

The development of a binding three-year sectoral PEP by all regions is the missing link between regional and *woreda* budget making, and consolidated sector envelop projections at the national level. This is clearly a long-term agenda. It will take SNNPR time to develop and implement the PEP approach and even more time for other regions to see the benefits of such a system.

Need to Boost Administrative Capacity at the Woreda *Level*

Compounding the problem of inadequate financing is weak local government capacity to deliver services. *Woreda* capacity has been improving, as more and more staff at the zonal and regional levels are redeployed to the *woreda*s and training programs for local level staff are completed. Despite progress, however, lack of sufficient capacity remains as one of the key obstacles to improving services to achieve better outcomes in social sectors.

This problem assumes three forms. One is the lack of complementary infrastructure (water, electricity, phones) and equipment (vehicles, computers) to raise staff productivity. Another is the shortage of trained staff. Many *woreda*s report having too few people to perform tasks that would improve their efficiency. The *woreda*s are short on managerial talent; frontline professionals (teachers, doctors, nurses, water specialists); and people with specialized skills in procurement, financial management, and accounting and reporting.

The problems posed by these skill shortages are compounded by weak support systems. While streamlining of *woreda*-level financial management and accounting is under way and regions are moving toward a system of payments for all *woreda* offices through a single treasury system (Box 5.2), timely and complete reporting remains a challenge. Accounting and financial reporting is manually performed at the *woreda* level, even in SNNPR, the most advanced region with regard to expenditure management and control reforms; this slows the sharing of financial information. At the *woreda* level, sector managers yearn for simple and robust management tools, such as a basic information sheet for each sector that combines physical and financial data in a simple summary that allows finance and sector managers to monitor budget execution and its impact during the year. Currently, there is no easy way to translate detailed data on budgets and expenditures into summary information on

---

Box 5.2. Improving Financial Management Reporting at the *Woreda* Level

---

Once the *woreda* budget is notified, sectors may request adjustments once a year. All such adjustments, including requests to transfer resources from one line item to another within the same category of expenditure (for example, recurrent non-salary), are supposed to be approved by the *woreda* Cabinet.

Woredas follow the rules for budget transfer at the regional and federal level. These rules do not allow transfers from non-salary to salary budgets or from the capital to the recurrent budget. Authorized adjustments are supposed to be made only after review of the first six months of budget execution. *Woreda* Cabinets are reportedly actively monitoring budget execution and supervising sector offices' implementation of their plans as a basis for such adjustments.

Streamlining *woreda*-level financial management is under way in all of the regions visited. In SNNPR all financial management tasks have been reorganized under the *Woreda* Office of Finance and Economic Development (WOFED), which "serves" all other *woreda* offices (single treasury system). WOFED receives sector offices' budget release requests for the coming month and notifies them of their monthly envelop. Thereafter it performs all financial transactions necessary for sector offices to perform the activities planned for the month. This system was adopted in 2004/05; hence, it is too early to assess whether it serves offices well. The concentration of financial management expertise should facilitate timely and complete financial management reporting.

Source: Dom (2004).

---

financial performance (on a sector by sector or program by program basis). No formal mechanism is in place through which regional Bureaus of Finance and Economic Development provide regionally consolidated sectoral financial performance to sectoral bureaus, although in regions where the expenditure management and control reforms are sufficiently advanced (such as SNNPR), officials have indicated a willingness to establish such mechanisms.

With decentralization at the *woreda*-level in 2002/03, the number of staff at the *woreda* level increased dramatically. In Oromiya, for example, the number of *woreda*-level staff (excluding teachers and health professionals) rose 54 percent (Table 5.2).

Table 5.2. Number of Regional and *Woreda*-Level Personnel in Oromiya Before and After Decentralization

Item	2001/02 (actual)	2004/05 (plan)	Percent Increase
Regional level	3,090	3,340	8.1
Woreda level	49,591	76,151	53.6
Teachers	50,880	50,880	0
Health workers	6,519	6,519	0

Source: Mussa (2005a).

The devolution of responsibility to the *woredas* has significantly increased demands for staffing *woreda* administrations, bureaus, and frontline services. Four years into the *woreda*-level decentralization, a large number of positions remain vacant (Tables 5.3 and 5.4). The GTZ-Selam Development Consultants (2005) *Woreda*-Municipality Benchmarking Study indicates that up to 25 percent of positions in six *woredas* in Oromiya remained unfilled in

2005. The problem appears acute in Tigray and SNNPR. A study by Adal (2005) of four *woreda*s indicates that: (i) in Harshin *woreda*, Somali region, the capacity building office had just 11 percent of the employees it needed, and the *woreda* had just 50 percent of the teachers and 14 percent of the health office staff it needed; (ii) in Bolosso Sorre *woreda*, in SNNPR, the health sector had only 60 percent of the staff it needed; and (iii) in Delanta Dawnt *woreda*, Amhara region, education offices had just 39 percent and the health offices only 29 percent of the staff needed.

A recent review of the civil service (Mussa 2005c) concludes that the reasons for severe staff shortages include unattractive work environment/location (remoteness and lack of services, amenities, and opportunities); low pay; and the shortage of qualified personnel in the market. The study indicates that low salaries, the lack of fringe benefits, job dissatisfaction, and demand from outside the civil service are among the factors affecting staff shortages.

Table 5.3. Staffing in Sector Offices in Delanta Dawnt *Woreda*, Amhara Region, 2003/04

Sector Office	Positions Approved	Positions Budgeted	Positions Vacant	Percent Vacant Positions
Capacity building	57	29	28	49
Education	27	25	2	7
Health	14	5	9	64
Woreda administration	38	26	12	32
General administration and security	4	3	1	25
Woreda court	26	24	2	8
Justice	8	4	4	50
Agriculture and rural development	264	143	121	46
Information	39	23	16	41
Finance and economic development	34	16	18	53
Mass organization and participation	6	2	4	67
Youth, culture, and sport	17	3	14	82
Small-scale industry	3	2	1	33
Police	10	5	5	50
Prisons	11	11	0	0
Total	558	321	237	43

Source: Adal (2005).

The study notes the traditions of stability of tenure and risk aversion in the Ethiopian civil service system. That situation is changing, however, and turnover is now high. Turnover and scarcity of staff are high in those professional and technical areas where supply is low and demand high, particularly in the health and water sectors.

One of the staff deployment strategies of decentralization was to transfer 40–60 percent of regional staff to the *woreda*s. Doing so has proved problematic. Staff have been

Region	Woreda	Total Staff	Vacancies	Percent Vacant Positions
Table 5.4. Staff Vacancies in Selected *Woredas*				
Amhara	Fogera	1,175	221	19
	Habru	1,084	184	17
	Kutaber	871	209	24
	Sekela	693	109	16
	Sekota	957	257	27
	Weldia	490	64	13
	Total	**5,270**	**1,044**	**20**
	Mean	**878**	**174**	**20**
Oromiya	Boji	715	178	25
	Cheliya	789	222	28
	Gubakorcha	702	340	48
	Guduru	714	149	21
	Kurfa Chele	637	121	19
	Mettu	522	47	9
	Total	**4,079**	**1,057**	**26**
	Mean	**680**	**176**	**26**
Tigray	Gulomakda	785	62	8
	Kafte Humera	644	39	6
	Kelete Awlaelo	612	8	1
	Laelaye Adiyabo	607	114	19
	Atsbi Womberta	635	10	2
	Total	**3,283**	**233**	**7**
	Mean	**657**	**47**	**7**
SNNPR	Basketo	404	98	24
	Kedida Gamila	1,461	4	1
	Konso	1,163	188	16
	Kucha	574	228	40
	Shebedino	1,218	104	9
	Yiregachifee	263	50	19
	Total	**5,083**	**672**	**13**
	Mean	**847**	**112**	**13**
Total for all regions		**17,715**	**3,006**	**17**
Mean for all regions		**770**	**131**	**17**

Source: GTZ-Selam Development Consultants (2005).

reluctant to go to the *woreda*s, where career ladders are less attractive than at higher levels of government. The structure is inadequate, particularly for the positions opened, to absorb qualified and highly paid personnel. Attempts have been made to attract and retain staff, including offering them priority in training, establishing hardship allowances, creating a system of differential rates for counting service years, and offering contractual or temporary employment.

The GTZ-Selam Development Consultants (2005) Benchmarking Survey identifies three main causes for the failure of the *woreda*s to recruit sufficient numbers of staff: low attractiveness of the location, particularly in remote areas; unattractive salary; and the lack of candidates who met the criteria for the jobs with open vacancies.

Need to Improve Personnel Management of Frontline Service Providers

Personnel management and compensation policies of frontline providers are key to the success of service delivery reforms. But personnel management is one of the least developed areas in the region-to-*woreda* decentralization. This challenge has to be addressed urgently to avoid slowing the momentum of decentralized service provision.

One of the most important issues raised by decentralization is which level of government is responsible for deploying teachers and health staff. Currently, responsibility for teacher deployment is shared by the regional government and *woreda* administrations. Regional Bureaus of Education recruit teachers with degrees (for secondary schools) and teachers with diplomas (for Grades 5–8), whom they deploy to *woreda*s, in principle according to the *woreda*s' requests. *Woreda*s recruit and deploy teachers for Grades 1–4 themselves.

Similar shared and overlapping responsibilities exist in the deployment of doctors, health officers, and nurses. About 20,000 health extension workers will be trained and posted to *woreda*s throughout the country between 2004 and 2009. While the activities for which these health extension workers are recruited are clearly the responsibility of the *woreda*s, their training and deployment is an initiative of the federal government (Dom 2004).

There is general agreement on the desirability of increasing the deployment of teachers and health workers to *woreda*s to make progress toward national goals, such as improving school quality and obtaining better balance of personnel between rural and urban areas. Responsibility for managing the personnel, much less financing their deployments, is not clear, however.

Salary scales and promotions are handled by the region. In principle, *woreda*s have discretion to set salaries; in practice they often adopt the scales and guidelines of he regions and federal government. Shedding staff remains difficult, and the *woreda*s often have to confer with the regional authorities to take such actions.

Turnover of teachers is high, threatening the operation of schools and the improvement of school quality (JRM Education 2005). In Oromiya teachers typically remain on the job for a maximum of just four to five years. In many schools a third of all teaching positions remain vacant and a significant percentage of the staff, particularly in the second cycle of primary school, is under-qualified. In SNNPR while nearly 95 percent of the teachers in the first primary cycle are certificate holders, one-third of all teachers in the second cycle are under-qualified, and the figure rises to two-thirds in secondary schools.

The efficiency of deployment of staff across schools and health facilities needs to be addressed. A recent analysis (World Bank 2005a) finds that teachers are often deployed randomly, that is, based on factors other than school enrollment. The study using 2001/02 data indicates 41 percent randomness in teacher deployment in SNNPR; 8 percent in Tigray; 22 percent in Amhara; and 28 percent in Oromiya. The low figure for Tigray is comparable to that in the best-performing countries, suggesting that practices in the region may hold lessons for other regions on ways to manage the deployment of teachers. The findings for the country as a whole, however, suggest that the management of teacher deployment is weak, not only across schools but also between the two cycles of primary schooling within schools. These results are consistent with the reality that while teacher deployment rules may exist, outcomes are often decided at the local level by officials who ultimately implement rules in response to the priorities they perceive.

The health sector suffers from high rates of attrition and turnover. Two major reasons for this are poor working conditions and weak enforcement of staff policies. In principle, most nursing and medical students are funded by the government (Federal and regional) and required to fulfill a service contract of specified duration (usually three to four years). They are posted to service centers on the basis of a lottery, which in theory cannot be influenced, except for medical reasons. In practice, there are questions as to whether this process is done in a genuinely unbiased manner, and there are allegations that the lottery may be subject to manipulation (see below).

A survey of final-year nursing and medical students around the country reveals that 51 percent believe that a first posting is determined primarily by personal contacts, 56 percent believe they can get an undesirable first posting changed, and 43 percent admit that they may look for a job outside the health sector because pay and opportunities are better (Serneels and others 2004—see Figure 5.5).[14] In a study based on focus group discussions in Addis Ababa and four provincial towns, participants generally believed that the lottery system for posting new graduates is "corrupt and that assignments are not truly random" (Lindelow, Serneels, and Lemma 2004). They believed that individuals with the right connections are able to turn down their initial assignment and wait for a better one; that there are cases where students have swapped their postings, sometimes with an accompanying financial transfer; and that many prospective health sector workers find that they earn too little and therefore often leave the sector.

The findings of such surveys and studies should be interpreted with care because people's perceptions about a situation—especially as communicated in interviews—do not always reflect the reality of what is taking place on the ground. Furthermore, focus group assessments are neither objective nor representative, by design. Nevertheless, the findings of the survey and the focus group study that have just been described raise questions that need to be answered. At the very least, they point to the need for government action in undertaking an in-depth and critical review of the situation.

Significant premiums are needed to attract nurses and doctors to rural areas. Eighty percent of medical and nursing students report that they would take up a rural post for wage premiums of 43–60 percent above the urban rate. Yet, according to regressions done using data from the 2001 Child Labor Force Survey, there is no rural wage premium; doctors and nurses in rural areas were found to earn less than those in urban areas, after controlling for other factors such as the level of education. These results are based on data collected a few years ago, however, and some steps are being taken to address the situation, as described in the next section.

All of these problems are compounded by a degree of "brain drain" of qualified people away from the public sector and to the private sector, or outside the country. Substantial additional investment in human resources will be needed to reduce this, and to address

---

14. The survey included a total of 219 nursing and 90 medical students in eight institutions all over the country (Addis Ababa University; Gonder University in Amhara; Jimma University in Oromiya; Asella Nursing School in Oromiya; Yirgalem School of Nursing in SNNPR; Selihorn Nursing School in SNNPR; St. Luke's Catholic College in Oromiya; and Medco Biomedical College in Addis Ababa).

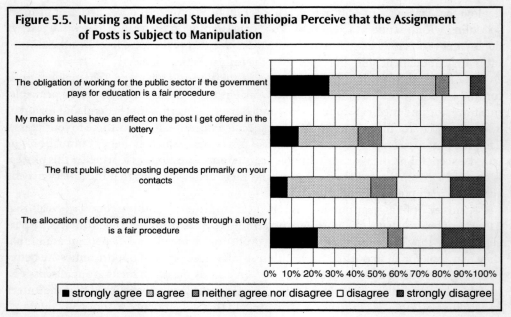

Figure 5.5. Nursing and Medical Students in Ethiopia Perceive that the Assignment of Posts is Subject to Manipulation

Source: Serneels and others (2004).

some of the other problems mentioned above such as the low wage premiums currently earned by workers in rural areas. This investment is especially needed at the regional and *woreda* levels, reinforcing the need for much more block grant resources to be passed down from the Federal government to the regions, as discussed above.

Regional Innovations for Recruiting and Retaining Workers

Regional governments have been testing innovations for recruiting and retaining different categories of employees (Mussa 2005a, 2005b). In Oromiya salary and non-salary incentives are offered in remote *woreda*s which are facing difficulties in retaining staff. The region has already begun introducing new incentive mechanisms for teachers and health professionals where staff turnover is high. Among the planned incentives is the possibility of transferring professional staff from remote *woreda*s to more urban areas after a certain period of service. The region is also adopting the federal government's policy that provides a 20–40 percent hardship allowance in *woreda*s with severe climatic conditions. In this regard, the region has been paying 20–30 percent of salary as hardship allowance to all personnel in 20 *woreda*s. There is some demand for hardship allowances to be paid in some other *woreda*s as well. The Region is working to respond to this demand phase by phase.

In the Tigray region, there have been proposals to introduce a fast-track career mechanism for certain types of public employees. As an incentive to staff, capacity building programs for *woreda* sector offices—distance education and regular education at the diploma, BA, and MA levels—were introduced. To ensure that staff enrolled in regular education programs at regional and national universities return, they are required to sign an agreement that obligates them to serve for a given number of years to compensate for the cost of their education.

In 2003/04 some *woreda*s in the region introduced an incentive mechanism for school teachers. Based on performance of the schools, the teachers receive a bonus at the end of the year. The scheme has enhanced competition between schools.

The Amhara region provides allowances for teachers, health professionals, and construction workers. For health professionals, "responsibility allowances," which range from Birr 50 per month for head nurses to Birr 200 for medical directors, were introduced in 2001/02. Teacher allowances have been provided since 1998/99. They range from Birr 90 for a head teacher in a first-cycle primary school (Grade 1–4) to Birr 125 for a head master of a teacher-training center. In 2001/02, the allowance for construction engineers was increased by about 40 percent of the previous professional allowance. Personnel based in remote and disadvantaged *woreda*s also receive priority in obtaining training opportunities.

In SNNPR the staffing structure stratifies *woreda*s into four categories, based on the degree of hardship. In 2003/04 incentive mechanisms were introduced for 9 climatically harsh *woreda*s and 17 disadvantaged *woreda*s. The incentives include the following:

▪ *Hardship allowance for nine climatically harsh woredas.* Allowances of 40 percent of salary are given to all employees in the five *woreda*s with the worst climate; allowances of 35 percent of salary are given to all employees in four other *woreda*s. All medical coverage is provided for employees working in the nine *woreda*s and their families. Workers in these *woreda*s also "receive" two extra years of service on top of their actual number of years of service.

▪ *Incentives for professionals in 17 disadvantaged and 9 climatically harsh woredas.* Professionals receive three-step salary increases, 100 percent medical coverage for themselves and their family members, and two extra years of service on the top of their actual number of years of service.

▪ *Training opportunities for health workers and teachers in remote woredas.* Some employees receive opportunities to pursue BA and MA studies. Employees sign contracts with the civil service to ensure that they return to work after they complete their studies and serve for as long a period as they spent at a college or university.

In December 2006, the Ministry of Capacity Building issued guidelines for the regions on how to ensure appropriate allocation and retention of staff, especially with regard to rural and hardship areas. These include: (i) guidelines on the amount of additional allowance for civil servants in hardship areas (e.g. 30 percent to 40 percent on top of salary for those in hot climate areas; 10 percent additional for those in cold climate areas); and (ii) priority to be given to employees that have remained for three years or more in hardship areas, in decisions regarding transfers of employees. The four larger regions have agreed to these guidelines.

Empowering Citizens and Communities to Improve Services and Outcomes

Given the crucial position of the *woreda*s in the service delivery chain, the functional relationships between the *woreda*s and the regional and Federal governments have to be strengthened and more clearly defined. The starting point should be a clearer definition of specific, well-defined outcomes the *woreda*s are expected to achieve and the provision of greater assistance from the regional and Federal governments in terms of funding and capacity building. But the benefits of decentralization will not be maximized unless another crucial group—citizens, the community, users of services—is pulled into the accountability mechanisms.

Ethiopia's development framework (the Sustainable Development and Poverty Reduction Program) and discourse espouse the spirit and language of participation. Citizens are acknowledged as playing a crucial role in mobilizing their communities, holding local governments accountable, and accelerating the process of democratization. Official pronouncements are matched by numerous local organizations, including community-level organizations, in the education, health, and water sectors.

For the social sectors, the most advanced and detailed proposal for involving citizen participation in service delivery was prepared for the education sector (see Government of Ethiopia 2002). The proposal provides a road map for decentralizing education management down to the school level and identifies the roles of all actors in the sector, starting with the Federal Ministry of Education down to the *woreda*-level education offices; Kebele Education Training Boards; and communities, teachers, and students. Among the more radical proposals in the guidelines are those that call for *woreda*s to provide block grants to schools, in order to encourage competition between schools and reward well-performing schools; and also to communities, to encourage them to participate actively in school management.

Before the start of decentralization, the role of citizens was one of the weakest links in the chain of service delivery in Ethiopia. One of the rationales for decentralization was to strengthen the role of citizens. Within the decentralized system, the kebele council is the forum where citizens could play a role in enforcing accountability of service delivery. However, the system is still evolving and initiatives to further strengthen this formal channel of citizens' participation should be welcomed.

There is mounting evidence, including within Ethiopia, that huge gains in outcomes can be made if citizens' roles are enhanced through participation and provision of information and choice. The role of the kebele councils is being strengthened by efforts—with participation by all levels of government in Ethiopia—to enhance transparency and accountability as part of the Protecting Basic Services operation. These efforts include initiatives to post *woreda* and regional budgets in public places, and to present budgets in formats that are readily understood by citizens.

The results of recent micro-studies provide insights into the extent of community participation in service delivery in Ethiopia. The role of citizens and communities is expressed through three main avenues: direct financial or in-kind contributions toward the establishment or maintenance of a facility, management of schools through the PTA or payment of teachers, and citizen voice in the local kebele and *woreda* councils, to balance the local executive political leadership and ensure that service providers are accountable to the community.

Findings from a recent micro-survey of *woreda*s in Amhara, Oromiya, and SNNPR show that in general communities are willing to contribute to primary education (Mussa, Dinku, and Abdo 2005). In Amhara communities have made substantial contributions toward expanding education by building and rehabilitating schools. Data from the Regional Education Bureau indicate that the total amount of community contributions has increased considerably in recent years. According to the bureau's annual report for 2004/05, community contributions in that year totaled about Birr 118 million (Birr 39 million in cash, Birr 52 million in labor, and Birr 27 million in materials), up significantly from 2003/04, when community contributions totaled Birr 26 million. The contributions were used to build new schools, satellite rooms, classrooms, fences, and teacher housing, and also to fund the purchase of school furniture. Community contributions represented roughly 19 percent of the total primary education budget for the region in 2004/05.

In areas of Oromiya where Basic Education Strategic Objective (BESO) programs operate, communities built 2,515 new classrooms and rehabilitated another 2,575; constructed 110 new and rehabilitated 1,220 teachers' houses; hired 1,917 teachers; and contributed in other ways—with contributions totaling Birr 46 million across the region in 2003/04. This is equivalent to Birr 12.7 per student—a non-negligible sum, given that the Government of Ethiopia's (2002) guideline suggests that *woredas* should provide the equivalent of Birr 10 per student as a government contribution to meet elementary school operational costs (Dom 2004).

In Bure *woreda* in the Amhara region, once parents and other community members agreed on the need for contributions to expand their schools, the amount of the contribution per household was left to be determined by individual families. Contributions are collected based on individual pledges. Parents contribute Birr 10–200 per school year, purely on a voluntary basis. Very poor families are exempted from contributing, as they are in other regions. Within a kebele, about 10 percent of residents decline to contribute, for various reasons.

In the Lay Gaynt *woreda* in the Amhara region, minimum rates were determined in advance and collected accordingly. The amount of contribution was between Birr 5 and Birr 10 per school year. Very poor households and the landless were exempted from any kind of contribution. In both cases, contributions for education were linked to participation in food and cash for work schemes, and participants were expected to make their contribution before collecting their wages.

The types of contributions from communities are exemplified by two *woredas*, Boset in Oromiya and Boritcha in SNNPR. In Boset, it was found that communities and parents made considerable contributions (in cash and kind) for a new school building; expansion and rehabilitation of existing schools; construction and rehabilitation of office rooms and residential units for teachers, fences, latrines, and other structures. In a few cases, contributions also paid the salaries of school guards, assistant teachers, and facilitators.

The amount of the contribution per household in Boset depends on various factors, including budget requirements for planned activities and community capacity. In most cases, parents and community members collectively determine the minimum amount of cash contributions per household (not per student). The contribution thus varies across households, kebeles, and *woredas*.

Communities also hire teachers locally when there is a shortage of teachers, and salaries can be negotiated between the communities and the teachers. Although Boset is a food-insecure *woreda* in Oromiya, the community has shown a willingness to contribute (Table 5.5). In 2004/05, 22 first-cycle primary schools were constructed and about 64 teachers hired and paid by the community. In primary schools where the *Woreda* Education Office could not hire teachers due to budget constraints, the community discussed and decided to hire teachers. In 2004/05 the *Woreda* Education Office hired 64 qualified teachers on behalf of the communities, for a total of Birr 128,000.

In addition, four first-cycle primary schools were built, at a cost of Birr 83,200, Birr 26,800 of which was covered by the community and the remaining Birr 56,400 of which was covered by UNICEF. The costs of other activities were paid for entirely by the community.

Table 5.5. Community Contributions to Education in Boset *Woreda*, Oromiya Region, 2004/05
(Birr, except where otherwise indicated)

Activity	Number	Total Cost	Cash	Labor	Material	Total
Construction of schools	4	83,200	12,000	4,800	10,000	26,800
Maintenance of schools	8	1,190	500	690	—	1,190
Expansion of classrooms	96	745,864	115,977	597,225	32,661	745,864
Construction of latrines	5	2,566	1,625	941	0	2,566
Payment of teacher salaries	64	128,000	128,000	0	0	128,000
Total						904,420
As percent of total *woreda* budget						16

Source: Mussa, Dinku and Abdo (2005).

In the Boritcha *woreda* in SNNPR, the expansion and maintenance of classrooms and the purchases of desks and other materials was funded entirely by contributions from the community (Table 5.6). The community also financed the purchase of stationery and duplicating paper for school exams, transport, and allowances. The contribution of communities in Boricha in 2004/05 is estimated at Birr 1.45 million Birr, or 19 percent of the *woreda* budget for education.

Another promising source of evidence of the benefits of citizen participation in service delivery comes from a local school management initiative currently underway in Amhara, Benshangul-Gumuz, and SNNPR. The program, currently in its second phase, is a collaboration between communities, *woreda* administrations, and USAID through an NGO called World Learning. The core objective of the program is to increase community ownership and management of primary schools by increasing effective participation of communities and fostering partnerships with local governments.

The most visible benefit of enabling citizen participation in the experimental program has been large financial and in-kind contributions for improving school conditions. These contributions are substantial: contributions to all 940 schools totaled $820,106 in 2004, almost four times the contribution (about $224,000) of the BESO project (Figure 5.6).

The substantial community financial contributions have been used to construct classrooms and pedagogical centers; improve infrastructure (desks, other furniture); and rehabilitate and build new teacher housing. These efforts have improved the quality of the schools, which has attracted more children and helped retain those already enrolled. The efforts have also increased school completion rates. Progress has been enhanced by campaigns by PTAs, Kebele Education Training Boards, and girls' advisory committees.

Girls' advisory committees in participating schools have helped increase girls' enrollment (Box 5.4). These committees educate the community on the value of girls' education and discourage early marriage and abduction of girls, which often deny girls the opportunity to complete schooling (Figure 5.7). The success of the committees has motivated some education officials to form them in schools that are partnering with BESO.

Community participation is also having the spillover effect of promoting local political support for the implementation of national policies, such as the MDGs. With

Table 5.6. Community Contributions to Education in Boritcha *Woreda*, SNNPR, 2004/05
(Birr, except where otherwise indicated)

Activity	Number	*Woreda* Education Office	Community Contribution			
			Cash	Labor	Material	Total Community
Construction of new schools	4	300,000	48,000			48,000
Expansion of school	90 rooms	0	270,000	32,400	48,600	351,000
Maintenance of school	20 rooms	0	30,000	36,000	54,000	120,000
Purchase of desks	1,125	0	21,094	25313	37965	84,375
Construction of housing for teachers	62	0	12,400	14,800	22,320	49,600
Construction of school fencing	15 km	0	15,625	18,750	28,125	62,500
Construction of pit latrines	18	0	13,500	16,200	2,430	54,000
Construction of library	10	0	2,5000	3,000	4,5000	10,000
Purchase of teaching materials	8	0	30,000	36,000	54,000	120,000
Purchase of blackboards	85	0	4,250	5,100	12,750	17,000
Creation of school garden	120 has.	0	49,800	0	0	49,800
Collection of water	20 pits	60,000	22,500	27,000	40,500	90,000
Total						1,056,275
Community contribution as percent of *woreda* budget						19

Source: Mussa, Dinku and Abdo (2005).

their enhanced roles in governance through participation and sense of empowerment, communities have taken part in monitoring the actions of frontline service providers. For instance, although communities cannot fire teachers, parents can and do report teachers who are absent or engage in socially unacceptable behavior to *woreda* education officials, who reflect these reports in teachers' performance records and evaluations (USAID/WLI 2004).

In the Arsi zone of the Oromiya region, communities are demonstrating the capacity to manage complex water projects. A key reason for the success of the water scheme is the active involvement of the community in managing the resource and the flexibility it has to levy fees and sell extra water outside the community (Box 5.5).

The Role of Communities in School Management

The active participation of communities through PTAs has helped increased enrollment rates and improved the enrollment and retention of girls. The BESO Programme illustrates how communities help in school management (see Box 5.3). PTAs are involved in planning and budgeting processes and in monitoring teaching. They deal with disciplinary problems of teachers and students and consult parents on a continuous basis about their children's school attendance.

As community organizations, PTAs are the driving force for community mobilization, participation, and contributions. A PTA typically consists of five parents and two teachers. To build the capacity of PTAs, which is weak, the *Woreda* Education Offices and the BESO

Box 5.3. Community Participation in Service Delivery at Work: Ethiopia's Basic Education Strategic Objective (BESO)

The program: The first phase of the Basic Education Strategic Objective (BESO I) was initiated in SNPPR, as the Community School Activity Program (CSAP). It targeted 720 schools between 1997 and 2000. The lessons learned from this phrase of the project were then scaled up to cover schools in two additional regions, Amhara and Benshangul-Gumuz.

The second phase (BESO II) began in 2002, as the Community Government Partnership Program (CGPP). By June 2004 the program covered 940 primary schools in 110 *woredas*. It is expected to cover 1,800 schools in the three regions before the end of the five-year second phase (2002–07).

How it works: The schools participating in the partnership are selected by the Regional Education Bureaus and *Woreda* Education Offices. Once they are identified, World Learning contacts the *Woreda* Education Office and the schools to begin a series of consultations that clarify the duration and objectives of the partnerships and the role of the community. Each school is in the partnership for a maximum of two years.

School incentive awards: Once a school joins the partnership, it receives an incentive award of about $1,500 paid over the two years that the school is in the partnership. The school incentive award is paid in three phases against completion of actions agreed on by the PTA and the community. The awards are provided to schools and communities to stimulate community involvement.

Strategic objectives: The strategic objective of the program is to strengthen local community support for primary education by increasing the effectiveness of PTAs and local education organizations, such as the Kebele Education Training Boards. This is done by strengthening the capacities of PTAs, the Kebele Education Training Boards, and the *Woreda* Education Offices; promoting alternative education by establishing non-formal education centers; using paraprofessional teachers and flexible timetables; and promoting equal access to schooling for boys and girls through campaigns discouraging early marriage for girls.

School development agents and zonal coordinators: A key instrument in building capacity and maintaining the sustainability of local participation in school management is the establishment of school development agents and zonal coordinators—experienced teachers or school directors who have been seconded to the World Learning Ethiopia office by the *Woreda* Education Offices or Regional Bureau of Education. Each school development agent works with at least 12 schools; each zonal coordinator is responsible for 10 *woredas* and 85 schools. The responsibilities of the school development agents include building the capacity of PTAs by identifying their training needs and delivering the necessary training, fostering community-government partnerships, developing programs geared toward building community ownership of schools, and motivating parents to send their children to school.

Source: Government of Ethiopia and AED/BESO II (2005a, 2005b).

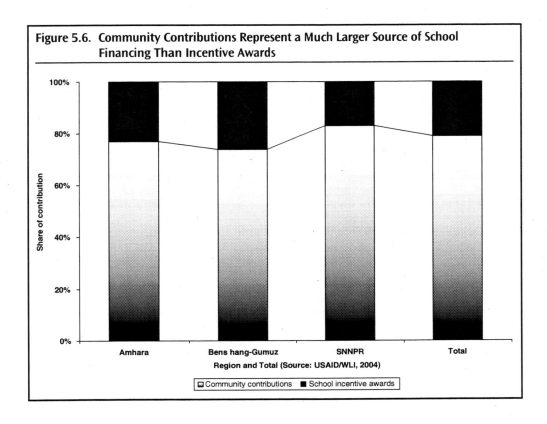

Figure 5.6. **Community Contributions Represent a Much Larger Source of School Financing Than Incentive Awards**

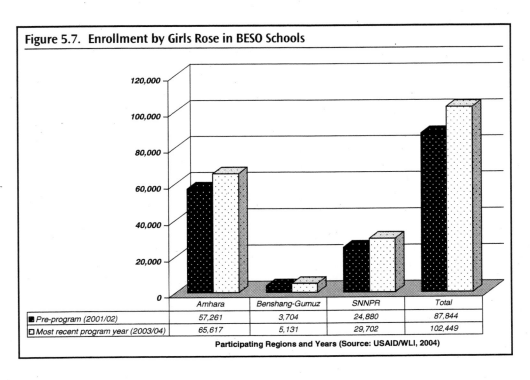

Figure 5.7. **Enrollment by Girls Rose in BESO Schools**

	Amhara	Benshang-Gumuz	SNNPR	Total
■ Pre-program (2001/02)	57,261	3,704	24,880	87,844
□ Most recent program year (2003/04)	65,617	5,131	29,702	102,449

Participating Regions and Years (Source: USAID/WLI, 2004)

Box 5.4. Boosting Girls' Participation in Primary Education Through Girls' Advisory Committees

---

To increase girls' enrollment rates, most schools in the BESO program have established girls' advisory committees. Using their local knowledge, these committees implement the most appropriate strategies for increasing girls' participation in their communities. Some activities are designed to increase participation, while others are geared toward empowering girls.

Activities related to increasing girls' participation include:

♦ Assessing the causes of low enrollment and educational performance by girls and designing appropriate interventions to improve them.

♦ Organizing community forums to disseminate information on the value of educating girls, and encouraging parents to send school-age girls to school and keep them there. The forums include influential people, such as religious, traditional, and political leaders. Home visits to households in the company of community leaders are also sometimes made.

♦ Providing tutoring and make-up classes for girls.

♦ Encouraging parents to reduce the amount of domestic chores girls must perform and to give equal support to boys and girls at home.

♦ Organizing school registration periods and, if necessary, extending them for girls.

♦ Providing public recognition of parents who send girls to school as a way to motivate others to do the same.

Activities related to empowering girls include:

♦ Providing moral support to girls and presenting them with awards for demonstrated progress.

♦ Arranging for class and school competition programs that involve girls, and presenting awards, in the presence of parents, to girls who do well.

♦ Providing continuous follow-up and encouragement through girls' advisory committees, women teachers, and other female professionals in the area.

♦ Assigning leadership roles to girls—as class monitors, school club leaders, and chairpersons in meetings.

---

project have conducted some training on planning; reporting; community participation and contributions; and record keeping.

The roles and responsibilities of PTAs vary across regions. In the Amhara region, PTAs are not responsible for managing the collection or use of the money contributed by the community. In contrast, PTAs in Oromiya and SNNPR are responsible for these activities. In most communities, only households with children in school are expected to contribute to the school, but some communities require all households to contribute. In some schools, the community contribution is counted on a per student basis, while in others it is counted on a per parent basis.

The Challenge of Community Participation in the Context of Decentralization

Community involvement in service delivery has been increasing in Ethiopia. Communities have a sense of ownership of their schools, and their contributions are large in financial terms, even compared with *woreda* budgets. Community participation in supporting local schools places a heavy burden on communities, however. Even in food-insecure *woredas*, participation is high, albeit not uniform across regions.

Box 5.5. Community Participation in Water Supply, Sanitation, and Health Education Schemes in Oromiya

---

The Hittosa water supply project is a joint project of WaterAid (an NGO), the water department of the Arsi zone, and the community of Hittosa. The scheme aims to provide safe drinking water for 28 villages and 3 small towns. Four other such schemes exist in the zone.

Each village forms an independent water committee, which works with an autonomous water management board at the *woreda* level. An executive committee coordinates the village committees and the water administration office. The communities contribute fees and labor to the scheme and are allowed to sell surplus water to other villages and users. The income and fees from the water sales are used to maintain the scheme and pay attractive and regular staff salaries. In return, employees provide reliable services and keep good records, especially of financial transactions. The scheme has worked because it is well designed, the leadership is responsible to the community, there is a well-established community structure and management system (water committees), and staff are motivated.

Source: Kassa (2003).

One of the main reasons for the increased burden on communities is the inadequate financing of local governments since decentralization. *Woreda* budgets are not sufficient to recruit teachers, maintain schools, and provide learning materials. With the growing trend toward greater community financing of these services, the capacity of communities is reaching its limit. It is becoming common, particularly in remote areas, for communities to contribute toward the construction of first-cycle primary schools; in some instances, they hire teachers locally and pay salaries. Since the continuity and sustainability of these salaries are not guaranteed, turnover is high, and *Woreda* Education Offices cannot replace such teachers, since the positions are not budgeted.

The drive to improve the quality and effectiveness of service delivery needs to fully take into account—given their scope—community contributions and participation in the planning and budgeting processes. It is essential to ensure that the burden is shared equitably across regions, *woreda*s and kebeles. The burden on disadvantaged communities, including food-insecure *woreda*s, should be reduced, with larger allocations of *woreda* resources. Clear guidelines should be established on how the burden should be shared by communities, *woreda* administrations, and other parties, including donors.

The role of community associations in promoting effective participation can be enhanced with training, as in the case of the BESO program. The training of PTAs is a key strategy for promoting community participation in the delivery of services.

Improving Services by Providing Information

Information is essential for assessing the performance of service providers and the actions of politicians and policymakers. It is crucial in making decisions about the benefits of a policy. Information also helps individuals make private choices about health, education, and water and sanitation.

Two key determinants of child health outcomes in Ethiopia are maternal knowledge and access to information. This conclusion is consistent with the finding of Christiansen and Alderman (2004), who show that maternal knowledge can explain much of the observed differences in child malnutrition. Unlike their study, which uses the education of the most educated female in the household, the new analysis done for this study using household data from the Welfare Monitoring Surveys of 1995 and 2000, matches children and their mothers, for the period 1995–2000. It uses year dummies to control for time variation in order to improve the ability to identify the effects of explanatory variables that are potentially endogenous in the cross-section. It is possible, for example, to conflate the effect of distance to a health center with preferences for health centers. If some parents have very strong preferences for using health clinics and therefore choose to live near a health center, the estimated effect of government intervention reflects those preferences as well. With a given distribution of preferences for health centers, expanding access to other areas may not generate similar effects. The advantage of time variation is that it allows the effect of changes in distance over time (that would occur through the opening or closing of health clinics) to be examined. By controlling for region and time (through the interaction of region and year dummies), this report identifies the determinants of health outcomes using within-region and over-time variation in the explanatory variables.

In the basic regression of child malnutrition, a literate mother can reduce her child's malnutrition by 0.5 standard deviations (23 percent) relative to illiterate mothers. One interpretation, derived from the health capital model, is that literate mothers face a lower cost of investment in health capital. Among mothers who report using health facilities, it is not education but the combination of education and information that generates the strongest impact on child health. A literate mother with access to information (as proxied by access to radio and television) increases her child's nutritional status by 15 percent.

Mother's education (measured by literacy) is the single most important determinant of child mortality. Literacy reduces infant mortality by 2.6 percentage points (nearly all of the reported deaths for the sample) and child morbidity by nearly 14 percentage points (34 percent). Mother's literacy matters more for boys than for girls, however, whereas the number of boys' deaths declines by 0.13 (9.3 percent), the number of girls' death falls by 0.09 (6.5 percent).

A second story that emerges is the role of internal pollution. Clean cooking oil has a consistently negative effect on child survival. Although not precise in the still birth regressions, the results suggest that the impact of clean cooking is of a similar magnitude as the effect of literacy. Like mother's literacy, clean cooking oil has a greater effect on boys than girls: indoor pollution has twice as great an effect on child morbidity among boys (−0.11, or 8 percent) than among girls (0.055, or 4 percent).

The Government's introduction of health extension workers into communities through the Health Extension Program is a way to improve household information about basic health inputs. The program focuses on the prevention of childhood and maternal diseases. It will be especially critical in implementing the Integrated Management of Childhood Illnesses (IMCI), which is being implemented in all regions as the key strategy for reducing under-five mortality and morbidity. The strategy supports interventions of the type considered in a recent note on reducing child mortality in the Lancet (Jones and others 2003). The results suggest that increasing maternal information and reducing internal pollution (through the use of clean cooking oil) may be fruitful strategies for reducing deaths among infants and children.

Improving Accountability Mechanisms

Communities make significant financial contributions to maintaining the continuity and quality of services in Ethiopia, participating directly in the management of the services, and offering specific solutions to difficult challenges (such as keeping girls in school). But citizen participation in Ethiopia is a weak link in the chain of service, primarily because there are no clear guidelines for communities' role and many communities lack information. Several sets of actions could improve citizen participation and involve citizens in service delivery in a more robust and effective way.

Institutionalizing Citizen Report Cards

Citizen report cards can be an effective way of enabling citizens to monitor the quality of services and the prudent and transparent use of resources (Box 5.6). They can help enforce agreements between the federal and regional government on the one hand and with the local government on the other. Regional governments can use *woredas'* scores on the report cards, together with other sources of information, to enforce performance contracts on specific targets.

Ethiopia currently lacks a mechanism for introducing, implementing, and publicizing the results of *woreda* report cards. A good beginning would be to scale up the recent activities of PANE, a consortium of NGOs, which has completed a report on a pilot citizen report card. This report assesses the performance of a sample of *woredas* in implementing the Sustainable Development and Poverty Reduction Program goals on education, health, and water and sanitation.

Strengthening Citizen Voice Through Other Social Accountability Mechanisms to Apply Social Pressures on Providers

Other promising approaches and mechanisms to enhancing clients' voice could also be tested in rural and urban environments Ethiopia. Several approaches that have been successful in some regions or in other countries could be piloted in selected *woredas* and kebeles and scaled up as experience grows. These include:

- Citizen monitoring of *woreda* performance indicators that have been agreed on with the regions (such as the performance agreements implemented in SNNPR— see Box 3.2).
- Community scorecards of school performance in coordination with PTAs.
- Citizen participatory planning and monitoring to strengthen the accountability of *woreda* and *kebele* councils for service delivery.

One of the key objectives of these mechanisms is to enhance community involvement in performance assessment and to coordinate channels of accountability to ensure better service delivery. This could also be achieved through the formal channel of the kebele where citizens are also represented in the council.

Box 5.6. Using Citizen Report Cards in Ethiopia

Citizen report cards allow users of public services to provide feedback to service providers regarding their performance. By identifying the key constraints (coverage, quality, reliability, and so forth) that limit their use of public services, citizens provide a clear message on the weaknesses of public services.

A pilot citizen report card in Ethiopia sampled 3,829 households in Afar, Dire Dawa, Oromiya, SNNPR, and Tigray. Dire Dawa was chosen as the representative urban subsample; only rural households were sampled in the other regions. Households were asked to assess key basic public services typically delivered by the *woredas,* including drinking water, health and sanitation, education, and agricultural extension services.

The report cards revealed the following key findings:

Drinking water

◆ Nearly three-fourths of all households lack potable water, and pollution of river water is a major concern.

◆ A significant proportion of respondents report that communities are involved in maintaining water sources. Most of this involvement is in the form of contributed labor.

◆ Many households express willingness to pay for improved water services.

Health and sanitation

◆ Most households report improvement in access to health care.

◆ Most households report that immunization services have expanded, but many cite lack of medicines, long distances, and poor quality of services as major reasons why they prefer private over public services.

◆ The cost of obtaining treatment in government facilities is high. Very few respondents who use public services report receiving free medicine.

Education

◆ Teacher absenteeism is low, and the quality of teaching is not a major concern.

◆ The shortage of drinking water and functioning toilets in schools is a major problem.

◆ Community involvement in school management is informal. Few parents belong to PTAs.

◆ The cost of education is significant and varies across regions. One-third of parents make extra payments to school administrators, and 17 percent of those paying extra fees report being coerced to do so.

Source: PANE (2005).

Launching Public Information Campaigns

Some key actions for improving education and health outcomes can be accomplished through public information campaigns. For instance, many children are out of school because their families do not permit them to attend, perhaps because they do not recognize the value of education. Child health outcomes could be improved substantially by providing nutrition information to mothers or helping households understand the value of boiling water, especially for children.

Public campaigns against smoking, drinking and driving, and unsafe sex have been successful in other countries. In Ethiopia the gains from public information—in health, in education, and in water and sanitation—would likely be large. *Woredas* and municipalities could use health extension workers in conjunction with community or municipal radios to disseminate information on child health and the value of education. Involving communities in the management of services in health, education, and water could increase accountability, improve ownership, and provide an avenue for transmitting information on specific issues, such as the value of girls' education.

Reducing the Opportunity Costs of Sending Children to School

Even if improvements in two of the key constraints—weak local government and inadequate citizen participation—occur, achieving the MDGs will not be feasible unless the huge opportunity costs facing poor households are removed or substantially reduced. These opportunity costs are evident in the tradeoff between income generating activities and the use of services.

Earlier studies (World Bank 2006b) indicate that about 45 percent of primary school–age children in Ethiopia work full time. Adding to this figure children who work part time pushes the rate of working children to 60 percent. Children of all ages participate in work, and the participation rate increases with age. When asked why their children work, 47 percent of parents reply by referring to high opportunity costs of sending their children to school. About 16 percent report that their children are not in school because they help with

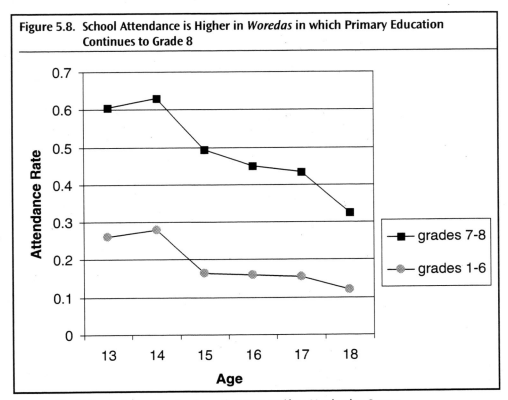

Figure 5.8. School Attendance is Higher in *Woredas* in which Primary Education Continues to Grade 8

Source: World Bank staff estimates from the 2000 *Welfare Monitoring Survey.*

domestic work. Another 14 percent report lack of a nearby school, 9 percent report that they cannot afford school, and 8 percent report that their children need to supplement family income. The significance of opportunity costs could be even larger than these figures indicate, because more than 80 percent of children report that they work in order to supplement household income or assist in household chores (Figure 5.8).

In 1994 the Government changed the structure of schooling from six years of primary education to eight. For a number of reasons (financial resources, political factors at the regional level, and so forth), the pace of change to the new structure was uneven across the country. Some communities adopted the new system quickly; others could not. In *woredas* where the full cycle of primary education is not available, children aged 13–18 years have lower attendance rates than children in *woredas* where eight years of primary education are provided. These results may indicate that parents whose children have little or no prospect of completing the full cycle of primary education have less incentive to send them to school.

High opportunity costs make it difficult for households to use and benefit from services. One consequence of high opportunity costs is child labor. Another is high child mortality and morbidity. Differences in the opportunity costs faced by households lead to inequalities in outcomes. If not addressed through public policy, these differences lead to persistent inequalities, which act as a drag on progress toward the MDGs.

APPENDIXES

Calculating Block Grants Allocations From Federal Government to Regions and Regions to *Woredas* Using the Three-Parameter Formula

From 2003/04 to 2006/07, a two-step allocation process was used to make Federal block grant allocations across regions. First, each region would obtain the same recurrent allocation as in 2002/03; this would be a minimum allocation. Second, after making these initial minimum allocations, the "three-parameter" formula would be used to distribute additional resources across regions. This section describes this second step and the way in which the "three-parameter" formula was applied to this additional pool of resources. As explained in Chapter 3, starting from 2007/08, the Federal government is gradually shifting to the new "fiscal equalization" approach. The "three-parameter" approach has also been used in some regions to distribute block grant resources to *woredas*, but regions have also been generally shifting to other approaches. The material in this section also applies to the "three-parameter" approach as it has been applied by regions to calculate the size of block grant transfers to each *woreda*.

The "three-parameter" approach uses three parameters: population, level of development, and revenue collection effort.

The allocation to each locality (region/*woreda*) is based on the following formula:

$$ G_t = \left[\frac{Pop_i}{\sum\limits_{i=1}^{10} Pop_i} * w_1 + \frac{Dev_i}{\sum\limits_{i=1}^{10} Dev_i} * w_2 + \frac{\mathrm{Re}\,vper_i}{\sum\limits_{i=1}^{10} \mathrm{Re}\,vper_i} * w_3 \right] * 100 $$

where: (i) G_i is the percentage share of grant entitlement for locality i; (ii) Pop_i is the population of locality i; (iii) Dev_i is an Index of development level of locality i (with a higher value indicating a less developed locality; (iv) Re $vper_i$ is an index of revenue raising effort and sectoral output performance indicator of locality i; and (v) w_j are weights assigned to the indicators.

Key features:

■ The total available funding is in effect split into three portions—allocated respectively based on the "population," "development level" and "own revenue effort" of localities—with predetermined percentage shares of the total going to each (65 percent, 25 percent and 10 percent for the allocations from the Federal government to the regions).

■ The "population" portion is allocated across localities on an equal per-capita basis (e.g. if one locality has twice the population of a second locality, then it gets twice the allocation).

■ The "development level" portion is meant to address equity; it is allocated across localities such that less developed localities get larger allocations. The "own revenue effort" portion is allocated across localities such that those with greater revenues and sectoral performance get larger allocations.

■ The "development level" portion is independent of population size and locality size. So two localities with equal development level and own revenue collection effort would get equal *total* allocations, regardless of differences in population size.

■ Localities are free to use their total allocation in any way they choose, in theory. In practice, in some regions, *woredas* are given guidelines as to minimum shares that should go to capital spending.

For Federal allocations to regions, there is 100 percent "offsetting" of expected external donor funding (for specific projects) from block grant allocations. This works as follows: (i) The allocations to each region following the above three-parameter formula are made from a pooled basket of funds that consists of two types of funds: the total amount of (untied) block grant funding available, as well as the total amount of (tied) funding that is expected to be available for regional donor-funded projects. (With some exceptions, all donor funding to regions for specific projects are supposed to go through the Federal government.) (ii) The previous step gives the total allocation to each region, from untied block grant (Treasury) sources as well as from tied donor-funded sources for specific projects. The allocation of block grant (untied) Federal funding for each region is calculated by taking the total allocation to that region (as calculated from the formula), and subtracting from this the amount of donor specific-project funding for that region. In other words, there is 100 percent offsetting of external donor funding from block grant allocations. In the case of Federal block grant transfers to regions, there is no offsetting of each region's own revenue collection from the region's block grant allocation.

In the case of the transfers from regions to *woredas*, there is variation across regions in terms of what items are "offset" from block grant allocation. There are two types of items that are often fully or partially offset from the block grant allocation to each *woreda:* (I) the expected amount of (on-budget) spending that the *woreda* is expected to undertake from donor specific-project funding; and (II) the amount that the *woreda* is expected to collect in own revenues. Typically, there is full (100 percent) offsetting of item (II) from block grant allocations, following the procedure explained in the previous paragraph. There is variation across regions in the extent of offsetting of item (I)—see next paragraph.

In some regions, there is full offsetting (100 percent) of item (I) from the block grant allocation to each *woreda,* while in other regions there is partial (less than 100 percent) or no offsetting from block grant allocations. "Partial offsetting" means that a *woreda*'s block grant allocation is offset by a predetermined percentage share of its expected expenditure from donor funding for specific projects.

The principle behind the offsetting of specific-project spending is that the total entitlement of funding for each region (or *woreda* if applicable) should be determined by the block grant allocation formula, regardless of whether this funding is untied (in effect, in the form of block grants) or tied (as in the case of donor funding for specific projects).

Issues in the Application of the "Three-Parameter" Formula

The formula is not sensitive to the service delivery needs of different localities, possibly creating a disincentive to expanding service delivery. As an example, compare two localities with: (i) the same population, development level and own revenue effort, but where: (ii) one locality has substantially higher enrollment than the other, because of greater efforts made to increase enrollment. Both will receive the same per capita allocation and total allocation. However, spending per student in the higher-enrollment locality would likely be lower than in the other locality and thus would be less able to fulfill its needs. In turn, this allocation system may reduce incentive to enroll more students.

Small localities benefit disproportionately in per capita terms, in a manner that may not be equitable; a small and rich locality could get a larger per capita allocation than a large and poor locality. The "population" portion of the total available funding provides an equal per capita amount to all localities, and so any difference between localities in per capita allocations stems from the "development level" and "own revenue effort" portion. The "development level" portion is problematic because it provides an equal amount of funding to two different localities that are equally developed, even if one has a much larger population than the other. This implies a lower per capita allocation for the larger locality.

A large and poor locality will get a larger total allocation from the "development level" portion than a small but rich locality. But the per capita allocation of the large locality will often be less than that of the small one, even though the large region is poorer.

The per capita Federal block grant transfers to the regions in Table A1 illustrate this point. As an example, SNNPR—which has one of the highest regional poverty rates— received a much lower per capita transfer in 2005/06 than the relatively rich region of Harari, due to the low population size in Harari. Indeed, as Figure 3.2 in Chapter 3 shows, there is a very close inverse relationship between a region's population and its per capita Federal transfer from the Federal government.

One justification for this type of relationship is that there are fixed costs that every region has to face, such as the costs of maintaining a Bureau of Finance, a Bureau of Education, and so on. Another is that the cost of service delivery (and therefore per capita needs) is higher in regions with lower population density.

The upshot is that the "three-parameter" formula is being used to address these different objectives simultaneously. In particular, the "development level" portion is attempting to address equity concerns, fixed cost concerns, and possibly the greater costs of service delivery in less densely populated areas, in ways that do not meet these objectives.

Table A1. Per Capita Block Grant Transfers and Population

	Proportion of people living in moderate poverty according to 1999/2000 HICES household survey	Proportion of people living in absolute poverty according to 1999/2000 household survey	Population 2005/06 (millions)	2005/06 per capita transfer from federal government (Birr)
Tigray	78.9	61.4	4.28	118
Afar	70.1	56.0	1.37	181
Amhara	62.3	41.8	18.87	90
Oromia	60.6	39.9	26.18	79
Somali	65.2	37.9	4.27	101
Benshangul/Gumuz	70.6	54.0	0.62	312
SNNP	69.4	50.9	14.70	84
Gambella	71.1	50.5	0.24	547
Harari	42.0	25.8	0.19	441
Dire Dawa	52.6	33.1	0.39	254

The "Fiscal Equalization" and "Unit Cost" Approaches for Block Grant Allocations

General Descriptions and Comparison of the "Fiscal Equalization" and "Unit Cost" Approaches

Aside from the "three-parameter" approach, the report mentions two other approaches for allocating block grants to localities (regions/*woredas*), the "fiscal equalization" approach (which is currently partially used for allocating Federal block grant transfers to the regions, as explained in Chapter 3) and the "unit cost" approach (used by several regions, notably SNNPR until 2005/06, to allocate block grants to *woredas*). Over the next four years, the "fiscal equalization" approach will be gradually phased in for the allocation of Federal block grant transfers to regions; from 2010/11 onwards, these allocations will be based entirely on the "fiscal equalization" approach.

Although there are important differences between the "fiscal equalization" and "unit cost" approaches, they share some common principles:

- Both approaches are primarily "needs-based" in the sense that recurrent funding—which accounts for the bulk of total funding—is allocated in larger quantities to localities with higher demand and provision levels of public services (localities with higher "needs"). Recurrent funding allocations are made separately for each sector/subsector (primary education, secondary education, health, and so forth).

- In both approaches, capital funding is allocated in a more equity-oriented manner, with larger amounts provided to localities that are more "backward," in effect, those with lower amounts of capital stock related to public service provision (for example, less schools per capita, health posts per capita). The rationale is that these localities are most in need of additional funding so as to be able to accelerate investment in the appropriate types of capital stock, and to be thus able to "catch up" with other localities.

▓ Both approaches—in common with the "three-parameter" approach—make adjustments to take into account own revenue collections by the localities, but they do so in different manners (see below).

▓ Both approaches—in common with the "three-parameter" approach, and in keeping with the principle of "block" (or untied) grants—are merely methods for calculating the *total* amount of the block grant allocation to each locality. Ultimately, each locality is generally free to use its total amount of available funding as it wishes; it is not obliged to adhere to the sectoral sub-allocations used in the calculation of its total block grant allocation. (So if $x were allocated to a locality for recurrent spending on primary education, for example, actual spending on this subsector need not be $x.) There may, however, be a constraint imposed that *total* recurrent spending (across all sectors and subsectors) may not exceed the *total* recurrent allocation. In the case of SNNPR, there has also been the expectation that *woredas* and urban administrations must meet the targets agreed to in the performance agreements (see below), and must use their available funding accordingly.

The two approaches differ somewhat in the manner by which the above two principles are adhered to. With the recurrent allocations, a key difference lies in the assumptions regarding the unit cost of service delivery. With the primary education subsector, for example, for both approaches, recurrent funding is allocated based on the expected total primary enrollment of each locality (they are both "needs-based" in this sense). However:

▓ With the "fiscal equalization" approach, recurrent allocations are initially made to each subsector under the assumption of equal unit cost for all localities. (For example, recurrent allocations for primary education for the following fiscal year are such that each locality gets the same amount per student that is expected to be enrolled. The amount allocated per student is roughly equal to the total primary education expenditure across all localities, divided by the total primary enrollment.) However, at the end of the calculation process, the total block grant allocation is adjusted by a factor that depends on population and other variables, to correct for differences between localities in economies of scale and remoteness.

▓ With the "unit cost" approach as practiced in SNNPR until 2005/06, recurrent allocations to each subsector were made under the assumption that all *woredas* would achieve equal unit cost *in the longer run* (over several years). In the shorter run, the recurrent allocation to a *woreda* for a particular subsector and fiscal year was based on a target unit cost that was set somewhere in between the unit cost of that *woreda* in previous years and the regional average unit cost. The expectation was that *woredas* with higher-than-average unit costs should gradually lower their unit costs over time—and that *woredas* with lower-than-average unit costs should gradually raise their unit costs over time. In each successive year, the target unit costs across *woredas* would thus get closer and closer to each other, converging over time. The target unit costs were, in turn, computed from target values of "cost drivers" (see below).

With the "unit cost" approach as used by SNNPR, a "total sector ceiling" was applied to each subsector and sector. For each subsector/sector, allocations for each *woreda* were scaled up/down (usually down) so that they added up (across *woreda*s) to the total ceiling allowed for that subsector/sector, for that fiscal year.

There are also some differences between the two approaches in making capital allocations, even though both follow similar principles as outlined above. Even though the aim in both cases is to allocate more to localities that are "backward," there are some differences in how this is defined and measured.

Finally, the two approaches differ in the way by which they take into account own revenue collection, as follows:

- With the "unit cost" approach as practiced by SNNPR until 2005/06, the computations described above for recurrent and capital funding were used to compute the total allocation/entitlement to each *woreda* (*woreda*/urban administration), but this was not equal to the actual transfer. To derive the actual transfer level for each *woreda* for a fiscal year, the *woreda's* expected own revenue collection for that year was subtracted from its total allocation/entitlement. A *woreda's* expected own revenue for a fiscal year was, in turn, estimated from its actual revenue collected in previous fiscal years. The "three-parameter" approach also subtracts a *woreda's* expected own revenue from its total allocation to determine its actual transfer.
- With the "fiscal equalization" approach, a locality's expected own revenue is *not* subtracted from its total allocation to determine its actual transfer. Each locality's transfer is equal to its allocation (with the latter determined using the recurrent and capital allocation processes described above). However, adjustments are made to the total allocations to take into account differences in own-revenue-raising capacity. Allocations are adjusted downwards for localities with higher-than-average capacity to collect own revenues (for example, a larger per-capita tax base). For regions with lower-than-average capacity to collect own revenues, allocations are adjusted upwards. These adjustments are made independently of the *actual* amounts of revenue collected in previous years; they only take into account factors such as the size of the tax bases which determine the *capacity* to collect own revenue.

The treatment by the "unit cost" and "three-parameter" approaches of own revenues is problematic because it reduces localities' incentives to widen their tax bases and to otherwise improve own revenue collection. In effect, if a locality takes steps to improve its own revenue collection, it is raising expectations of its own revenue collection in future years, thereby reducing its block grant transfer from the higher-level (regional/federal) government in future years. In this respect, the "fiscal equalization" approach is superior since it does not reduce localities' incentive to collect own revenues. (With the "unit cost" and "three-parameter" approach, matters are worsened by the fact that, in many regions, local governments are not allowed to "keep" for themselves any own revenue collected in excess of their expected own revenue collection. This gives them almost no incentive to collect any surplus revenue.)

More Details on the Unit Cost Approach

This section describes key details of the "unit cost" approach as used in SNNPR until 2005/06. The "recurrent" portion of the total available block grant resources was allocated to *woreda*s according to recurrent needs calculated separately for each key sector (such as education, health, agriculture), and based on specific targets for each subsector for the following fiscal year (such as number of primary students to be enrolled, number of health posts to be managed). Starting from 2004/05 in SNNPR, these targets were set as part of "performance agreements" signed between districts and the region, whereby the district commits to attain the targets.

In each key subsector *s,* the recurrent allocation for *woreda i* was roughly given by

$$
\begin{bmatrix} \text{Recurrent Allocation to Woreda} \\ \text{i for Subsectors} \\ \text{(e.g. Primary Education)} \end{bmatrix} = \begin{bmatrix} \text{Performance Target for} \\ \text{Following Fiscal Year} \\ \text{(e.g. Primary Enrolment)} \end{bmatrix} \times \begin{bmatrix} \text{Target Woreda Unit Cost} \\ \text{(e.g. Target Woreda Expenditure)} \\ \text{Per Primary Student} \end{bmatrix}
$$

—with all of these three figures specific to each *woreda,* for every subsector, in every fiscal year.

As mentioned above, a *woreda*'s target unit cost for a fiscal year was set at a level somewhere in between the *woreda*'s actual unit cost in previous years and the regional average unit cost. Thus, target unit costs across *woreda*s would get closer and closer to each other in successive years, converging over time.

Target unit costs (for each district and subsector) were, in turn, computed from target values for "cost drivers"; "cost drivers" are key measures and ratios (such as the pupil-teacher ratio or PTR in the case of education) that determine the unit cost. These target "cost driver" values were set individually for each *woreda*, with different values set for each *woreda*. The chosen target values were clearly specified for each district; each *woreda* knew exactly how its allocations were computed and which target "cost driver" values were used in the computations.

The setting of target values for the "cost drivers" was based on the principle that, in the longer run, all *woreda*s should have the same values for "cost drivers" (for example, PTRs). (This would, in turn, ensure that all *woreda*s have the same unit costs in the longer run.) A *woreda*'s target value for a "cost driver" (for example, the PTR in the district) for a fiscal year was set somewhere in between actual values in previous fiscal years and the regional average value for this "cost driver." As in the case of the unit costs, the expectation was that *woreda*s with higher-than-average values for a "cost driver" (such as PTRs) should gradually take measures to lower these values, while *woreda*s with lower-than-average values for "cost drivers" should do the opposite. In each successive year, the target values for the "cost drivers" would thus get closer and closer to each other, converging over time.

In primary education, for example, the target *woreda* unit cost (target expenditure per primary student) was the sum of: (i) target teacher salary expenditure per primary student;

(ii) target non-salary expenditure per primary student; and (iii) target operational (non-salary) cost per primary student. The biggest of these is the target teacher salary expenditure per primary student, which was given by:

$$\left[\begin{array}{l}\text{Target teacher expenditure} \\ \text{per primary student}\end{array}\right] = \left[\text{target average teacher salary}\right] \times \left[\text{target PTR}\right]$$

Again, all of these target figures were set individually for each *woreda,* and they were *specific to each woreda, in every fiscal year.* Over time, the target values set for the average teacher salary and the PTR would converge across *woredas.*

Ultimately, of course, *woredas* were not obliged to meet their target values for the "cost drivers", unless specifically stated so in the performance agreements. Each *woreda*'s total allocation was transferred as a block grant, and it was free to use this funding as it wishes, the only expectation being that it should meet the performance targets (for example, for primary enrollment) that it had signed onto in the performance agreements. However, the target values for the "cost drivers" were explicitly stated to each *woreda,* and in practice each *woreda* had an incentive to try and meet them, regardless.

This can be illustrated by examining incentives regarding the *woreda* average teacher salary (ATS) and the *woreda* pupil-teacher ratio (PTR), key cost drivers. A *woreda* with higher-than-average ATS (i.e. ATS higher than the regional average) would get a target ATS that was lower than its own ATS. It was free to maintain an ATS higher than its target ATS, but doing so would require it to dig into funding allocated by the formula for other uses. This was unlikely to happen since most *woreda* tended to be strapped for resources.

By contrast, a *woreda* with lower-than-average ATS would get a target ATS that was higher than its own ATS. It would be given a funding allocation in accordance with the target ATS, which would be sufficient for it to start raising its own ATS to meet the target value (thereby raising teaching quality).

The rationale is similar in the case of the *woreda* PTR. A *woreda* was free to hire more than the number of teachers that was implied by its target PTR. Yet, doing so would require it to dig into funding allocated by the formula for other uses, which it was not very likely to do given the very limited amount of total resources available to most *woreda* with lower-than-average PTRs (too many teachers) thus had an incentive to gradually raise their PTRs.

Woredas with higher-than-average PTRs (too few teachers) on the other hand, had target PTRs that were lower than their own PTRs. They were given funding allocations deemed sufficient for them to hire a sufficiently large number of additional teachers, so as to attain their target PTRs.

Even with the larger funding allocations, the region believed that some *woredas* would not hire the additional number of teachers needed; and so the performance agreements—introduced in 2004/05—included the district PTR as a specified maximum target not to be breached. High-PTR *woredas* would thus, in effect, sign onto an agreement to hire enough new teachers so as to significantly reduce their PTRs. In this respect, the PTR differs from most other cost drivers, which are not stated in the performance agreements. The PTR appears in the performance agreements, but only as a maximum target that is not to be breached.

Rural *woredas* and urban administrations both received block grant resources from the region in SNNPR, but the allocations for each of these subgroups came from different pools. In making budget allocations, the region first decided how much funding to allocate to each of these pools, and how much to allocate to the regional bureaus. Next, the block grant allocations were made across urban administrations based on the total amount available from the "urban administrations" pool; a similar procedure was carried out for the "rural *woredas*" pool. The result was that there may have been some differential treatment of urban administrations versus rural *woredas*, which the region justified by pointing to urban-rural differences in the prices of goods and services and in the costs of living, among other things. Regardless, for many "cost drivers" such as the average pupil-teacher ratio, the aim was still to equalize them across (and between) rural *woredas* and urban districts.

Regression Results on Education Outcomes Before and After Decentralization

Table C1. School-Level Regressions Explaining Educational Outcomes Before and After Decentralization					
	Dependent Variable				
Independent Variable	Change in Grade 8 Pass Rate (%)	Change in Repetition Rate (%)	Change in Pupil-Teacher Ratio	Change in Pupil-Section Ratio	Change in Ratio of Numbers of Teachers to Sections
Grade 8 pass rate, 2000/01 (%)	−0.81 (−13.15)				
Repetition rate 2000/01 (%)		−0.8 (−35.26)			
Pupil-teacher ratio, 2000/01			−0.81 (−34.64)		
Pupil-section ratio, 2000/01				−0.54 (−32.7)	
Ratio of number of teachers to number of sections, 2000/01					−0.89 (−40.75)
Constant	66.24 (10.76)	9.67 (30.97)	52.6 (49.65)	32.7 (16.57)	0.93 (24.45)
Number of observations	373	2244	2244	2244	2244
R^2	0.7	0.58	0.78	0.38	0.64

Note: Dummy coefficients for each *woreda* are included but not reported. Dependent variables are changes between 2001 and 2004. Numbers in parentheses are t-values.

Table C2. *Woreda*-Level Regressions Explaining Educational Outcomes Before and After Decentralization

Independent Variable	Dependent Variable				
	Change in Grade 8 Pass Rate (%)	Change in Repetition Rate (%)	Change in Pupil-Teacher Ratio	Change in Pupil-Section Ratio	Change in Ratio of Numbers of Teachers to Sections
Grade 8 pass rate, 2000/01 (%)	−0.78 (−10.68)				
Repetition rate 2000/01 (%)		−0.33 (−6.6)			
Pupil-teacher ratio, 2000/01			−0.35 (−5.85)		
Pupil-section ratio, 2000/01				−0.16 (−3.23)	
Ratio of number of teachers to number of sections, 2000/01					−0.64 (−13.34)
Constant	57.84 (10.58)	4.66 (22.4)	22.4 (6.03)	12.6 (3.18)	0.76 (13.98)
Number of observations	123	123	123	123	123
R^2	0.46	0.23	0.48	0.08	0.76

Note: Each *woreda* is a unit of observation; the analysis uses data defined using "post-decentralization" boundaries (see the introduction to Chapter 4 for an explanation of this.) Dependent variables are changes between 2001 and 2004. Numbers in parentheses are t-values.

Estimating the Effects of Decentralization on the Delivery of Human Development Services in Ethiopia

To fully investigate the effects of decentralization on public services in Ethiopia, it is useful to start with outcome variables of interest and public expenditure. Did these variables change during the period in which decentralized took place? If outcome variables did not change, decentralization may not have been responsible for the effects often attributed to it. If expenditure did not change during the decentralizing period, it is possible that both the center and the periphery made identical choices or that the center did not really decentralize but only appeared to do so. Hence the first thing to do is to establish that reform did in fact lead to nontrivial changes in both outcomes and financial flows over the period in question. If they did, did they improve or deteriorate? How did expenditure patterns change following decentralization, both in aggregate and by sector? How were these changes related to changes in expenditure?

Three hypotheses were used to test the effect of decentralization on the delivery of human development services:

i. $\bar{O}_1 = \bar{O}_2$. This simple t-test determines whether the means of outcome variables, $\bar{O}$, changed in statistically significant ways over the period in question. The variables are subscripted by period, where 1 denotes 2001/02 (before decentralization) and 2 denotes 2002/03 (after decentralization). Significance implies that decentralization coincided with changes in outcome variables of interest, such as enrollment rates and Grade 8 test scores. Data limitations allowed this test to be performed only for the education sector.

ii. $\bar{E}_1 = \bar{E}_2$. This t-test determines whether the means of expenditures variables, $\bar{E}$, changed in statistically significant ways with decentralization. The variables are subscripted in the same way as above. National aggregates as well as disaggregated data for education, health, agriculture, administration, and own revenues, are examined.

103

iii. The differences in education outcome variables are set on the left-hand side of the equation to estimate the model

$$\Delta O_j = \alpha + \zeta \Delta E_j + \theta F_j + \delta S_j + \beta G_j + \varepsilon_j,$$

where the decentralization variable is $\Delta E_j = E_{2j} - E_{1j}$, that is, the degree to which decentralization changed education expenditure *woreda* by *woreda;* **F** measures resource availability at the *woreda* level; **S** is a vector of socioeconomic and demographic characteristics; and **G** is a vector of geographic characteristics, all indexed by *woreda j.*

If decentralization improved educational outcomes—enrollment rates and test results—by giving *woreda*s more discretion over greater resources, one would expect ζ to be positive and significant. But it is also possible that outcomes improved not due to higher expenditures but to better administration and targeting of a constant or lower level of expenditure.

Table D1 reports regression results that test the above hypotheses. *Woreda*-level primary subsector regressions using data from SNNPR for 2001 and 2004 were run with two dependent variables: (i) the change in gross enrollment rate (between 2001 and 2004); and (ii) the change in the Grade 8 examination pass rate. The main purpose is to examine the relationship of education outcomes with each of the following: (i) changes in spending; and (ii) changes in quantity of the main educational input, i.e. teachers. Only selected regression results are reported in the above table.

Regressions (1-a) and (1-b) report results with the change in the gross enrollment rate (GER) as the dependent variable. The relevant teacher quantity measure here is the number of teachers per 1,000 residents rather than the pupil-teacher ratio, which is an endogenous variable whose value would rise if the enrollment rate (the dependent variable) rises. Regression (1-a) shows that this variable is statistically significant and of the expected sign, implying that increased teacher quantity leads to improved enrollment rates.

In regression (1-b) where the GER is again the dependent variable, the teacher quantity measure is excluded, and a spending measure is included: the change in the total educational spending per capita. While a more appropriate measure would have been the change in per capita spending in just the primary subsector, this would have limited the number of observations substantially because a breakdown into primary versus other types of educational spending is not available for many *woreda*s. The regression shows that the percentage change in the spending measure is statistically and positively associated with the change in the GER, at 10 percent level.

Other independent variables in these regressions also provide useful information, suggesting that some groups of disadvantaged *woreda*s have experienced larger changes in GERs than others. The sign of the "distance from zonal capital" is positive and statistically significant, indicating large GER improvements on the part of remote *woreda*s, and confirms the findings from earlier descriptive analysis of improvements for the remote *woreda*s with decentralization. Another indicator of development level is the degree of road access of *woreda*s. The regressions show that *woreda*s that are disadvantaged in this regard—i.e. that have fewer kilometers of seasoned roads per capita than others—had stronger GER improvements than other *woreda*s.

Regressions (2-a), (2-b) and (2-c) provide results with the change in the Grade 8 pass rate as the dependent variable. The sample used is restricted to *woreda*s that started off with low pass rates to begin with—those whose average Grade 8 pass rate in 2001 was less than

Table D1. Effects of Changes in Expenditures on Educational Outcomes in the Primary Education Subsector: Results of *Woreda*-Level Regressions for SNNPR

	Change in Gross Enrollment Rate 2001–2004 (%)		Change in Grade 8 Percentage Pass Rate 2001–2004[2] (%)		
	(I-a)	(1-b)	(2-a)	(2-b)	(2-c)
Gross Enrollment Rate 2001	0.12** (2.74)	0.14* (1.86)			
Grade 8 Percentage Pass Rate 2001			−0.69** (−4.56)	−0.96** (−4.86)	−0.99** (−4.15)
Repetition Rate 2001					
Percentage Change in Total Education Spending Per Capita, 2001–2004		0.67** (1.97)		6.36** (2.50)	
Percentage Change in Primary Education Spending Per Primary Student, 2001–2004					1.46** (4.21)
Change in Pupil-Teacher Ratio, 2001–2004			−0.002* (−1.82)		
Change in Number of Teachers Per 1000 Residents, 2001–2004	8.16** (2.49)				
Change in Gross Enrollment Rate, 2001–2004				−0.04 (−0.14)	
Dummy for Food Insecure *Woredas*	1.51 (0.69)	1.55 (0.66)	5.99* (1.79)	9.35** (2.23)	8.11* (1.82)
Dummy for Pastoral *Woredas*	5.82 (1.30)	7.09 (1.22)	−2.17 (−0.45)	−6.93 (−1.35)	−2.02 (−0.22)
Dummy for Rural *Woredas*	2.72 (0.77)	6.20* (1.73)	5.11 (1.42)	8.83** (2.23)	
Distance from Zonal Capital (km)	0.024** (2.31)	0.02** (2.15)	−0.017 (−0.65)	−0.03 (−0.84)	−0.03 (−0.89)
Total Kms of Seasoned Roads in *Woreda*, Per 1,000 Residents	−9.1** (−2.38)	−8.7** (−2.37)	22.0** (5.14)	24.0** (4.55)	25.8** (3.77)

(*continued*)

Table D1. Effects of Changes in Expenditures on Educational Outcomes in the Primary Education Subsector: Results of *Woreda*-Level Regressions for SNNPR

	Change in Gross Enrollment Rate 2001–2004 (%)		Change in Grade 8 Percentage Pass Rate 2001–2004[2] (%)		
	(I-a)	**(1-b)**	**(2-a)**	**(2-b)**	**(2-c)**
Constant	1.55	−1.55	42.7**	53.6**	67.2**
	(0.33)	(−0.21)	(4.36)	(4.89)	(4.5)
Number of Observations (*Woredas*)	92	80	60	54	40
R-squared	0.39	0.3	0.47	0.46	0.47

*, **: statistical significance at 10 percent and 5 percent levels, respectively.
Notes:
1. OLS regressions reported with robust standard errors; t-statistics in parentheses.
2. The sample for the regressions with the change in the Grade 8 pass rate as the dependent variable was restricted to the *woredas* with an average Grade 8 pass rate of less than 80 percent in 2001.
3. All regressions use data only covering primary schools.
4. All regressions use data defined using "pre-decentralization" boundaries (see the introduction to Chapter 4 as well as Appendix 4.C for an explanation of this).

80 percent. The results support the case that pass rates are much easier to improve when they are already low.

The teacher quantity measure used here is the commonly used pupil-teacher ratio. Regression (2-a) shows that lower changes in Grade 8 pass rates are associated with larger changes in pupil-teacher ratios. Regressions (2-b) and (2-c) show a positive and statistically significant relationship between changes in Grade 8 pass rates and percentage changes in two different spending measures: total educational spending per capita and educational spending per primary student.

The Grade 8 pass rate regressions also show that two disadvantaged groups benefit, again: food insecure *woredas* and to some extent rural *woredas*. However, the *woredas* with greater road access apparently benefited more from changes in the pass rate than other *woredas*.

Methodology and Technical Details for Data Analysis in Chapter 4

The data used for the analysis in Chapter 4 were obtained directly from the regional governments of SNNPR and Oromiya. Data for 2001 and 2004 on the key variables were obtained at the *woreda* level. In addition, data were obtained for SNNPR at the primary school level, on test scores, number of teachers, number of students, number of sections and repetition rates.

*Woreda*s were classified as food-insecure if they had any food insecure households eligible for participation in the Productive Safety Nets Program or PSNP (regardless of what proportion of all *woreda* households were eligible). All food-insecure households are supposed to be eligible for PSNP food and cash transfers; as part of the PSNP, effort is spent on identifying food insecure segments of the population.

As mentioned in the introduction to Chapter 4, between 2001 and 2004 there were many cases where a *woreda* (which will be referred to below as the "mother *woreda*") split into two or even three—thus creating one or even two new localities with separate administrative boundaries. Each of these new localities (each referred to below as a "daughter *woreda*/urban locality") became either a rural *woreda* or an urban administration with *woreda* status. Urban administrations did not exist before decentralization to the district-level.

All quantitative comparisons between 2001 and 2004 were done using either "pre-decentralization *woreda* boundaries" or "post-decentralization boundaries," for both time periods. (The chapter specifies which approach was used for which portion of the analysis.) When "pre-decentralization boundaries" were used, it was necessary to aggregate 2004 data (for example, budget/expenditure data) for the "daughter" *woreda*s, so as to be comparable with the 2001 data for the "mother" *woreda*.

"Post-decentralization boundaries" were used only for comparisons of outcome data (for example, test scores, pupil-teacher ratios) between 2001 and 2004. To derive outcome data for 2001 when using "post-decentralization boundaries," it was necessary to compute outcomes for the geographical areas in 2001 that would later become the "daughter" *woreda*s in 2004. This was done by computing outcomes for the schools within each relevant geographical area. For example, between 2001 and 2004, Awassa *woreda* split into two parts: Awassa Zuria (rural) *woreda* and Awassa Town, the latter with its own separate urban administration. Computing outcomes for 2004 was straightforward; they were simply based on 2004 data for Awassa Zuria and Awassa Town. But computing outcomes for 2001 was less straightforward. To do this, it was necessary to use 2001 data and make separate computations for: (i) the schools that would become a part of Awassa Zuria by 2004; and (ii) the schools that would become a part of Awassa Town by 2004.

Several places in the chapter refer to the "coefficient of variation." The coefficient of variation of a distribution is simply the standard deviation of the distribution divided by the mean. The use of the mean in the denominator corrects for any scale effect, and makes it possible to use the coefficient of variation to compare the variability of two very different distributions. By contrast, the standard deviation is not comparable across different distributions, and (unlike the coefficient of variation) is not independent of the unit of measurement used.

References

Adal, Yigremew. 2005. A Study on the Implementation of the Decentralization Policy in Ethiopia. Addis Ababa: Oxfam.

Amhara National Regional State. 2005. "Intergovernmental Relationships: The Experience of the Amhara Regional State." Paper presented at the Government of Ethiopia-Donor IGR Workshop, March 23, Addis Ababa.

Central Statistical Authority (CSA). 2005. "Intergovernmental Relationships: The Experience of the Amhara Regional State." Presentation at the Government of Ethiopia-Donor IGR Workshop, March 23, Addis Ababa.

Christiansen, L., and H. Alderman. 2004. "Child Malnutrition in Ethiopia: Can Maternal Knowledge Augment the role of Income?" *Economic Development and Cultural Change* 52 (2):287–312.

Dom, Catherine. 2004. "Decentralized Policy-Based Budgeting for Education." Study prepared for the Joint Review Mission of the Education Sector Development Program, Addis Ababa.

Ethiopia House of Federation. 2007. "The New Federal Budget Grant Distribution Formula." The Secretariat of the House of Federation. May, Addis Ababa.

Government of Ethiopia. 2002. "Guideline for Organization of Education Management, Community Participation and Educational Finance." Ministry of Education, Addis Ababa.

———. 2005a. "Ethiopia: Fiscal Decentralization Strategy." Paper presented at the Government of Ethiopia-Donor IGR Workshop, March 23, Addis Ababa.

———. 2005b. "Ethiopia Fiduciary Assessment." Produced with Task Team funded by the UK Department for International Development and the European Union.

Government of Ethiopia and AED/BESO II. 2005a. "Second National Learning Assessment of Grade 4 Students." National Organization for Examinations and AED/BESO II, Addis Ababa.

Government of Ethiopia and AED/BESO II. 2005b. "Second National Learning Assessment of Grade 8 Students." National Organization for Examinations and AED/BESO II, Addis Ababa.

Government of Ethiopia/Ministry of Finance and Economic Development. 2005a. "Ethiopia: Building on Progress: A Plan for Accelerated and Sustained Development to End Poverty (PASDEP)." Addis Ababa.

———. 2005b. "Ethiopia Participatory Poverty Assessment 2004–05." Addis Ababa.

GTZ-Selam Development Consultants. 2005. "*Woreda*-City Government Benchmarking Survey Part II." Addis Ababa.

Halvorsen Tor and Robert L. Smith. 2005. "Delivery of Health and Education Services in Ethiopia: The Role of National Institutions." Presentation at the 8th Annual Norwegian Education Trust Fund Seminar. October 13th and 14th. Oslo, Norway.

Heymans, C., and M. Mussa. 2004. "The Ethiopia IGR: Intergovernmental Fiscal Reforms in Ethiopia: Trends and Issues." World Bank, Washington, D.C.

Joint Review Mission Report for Education. 2005. Addis Ababa.

Jones, Gareth, Richard Steketee, Robert Black, Zulfiqar Bhutta, Saul Morris, and the Bellagio Child Survival Study Group. 2003. "How Many Child Deaths Can We Prevent This Year?" *Lancet* 362 (July).

Kassa, Adane. 2003. "Hittosa Water Supply, Sanitation and Health Education Management, Arsi Zonal Administration, Oromiya Regional National Government, Ethiopia." Addis Ababa.

Krishnan, P. 1996. "Private and Social Rates of Returns to Schooling." PHRD Study 9. Oxford CSAE, Oxford University, Oxford, UK.

Lindelow, M., P. Serneels, and T. Lemma. 2004. "The Performance of Health Workers in Ethiopia: Results from Qualitative Research." World Bank, Washington, D.C.

Mussa, M. 2004. "A Study of Capital Budget Utilization in the Education Sector." Joint Review Mission 2004 Preparatory Study. Addis Ababa, Ethiopia.

———. 2005a. "Progress of Decentralization and Capacity Building Programs in Oromiya Region." Addis Ababa.

———. 2005b. "Progress of Decentralization and Capacity Building Programs, SNNPR." Addis Ababa.

———. 2005c. "Civil Service Employment and Pay in Ethiopia." World Bank, Washington, D.C.

Mussa, M., Dinku, and Abdo. 2005. "Community Participation in Primary Education." Report to the Joint Review Mission for Education 2005. Addis Ababa.

PANE (Poverty Action Network of Ethiopia). 2005. "Pro-Poor Services in Ethiopia. A Pilot Citizen Report Card." Addis Ababa.

Resal Ethiopia. 2001. "Public Expenditure Management Aspects of Food Security." Final Report. Addis Ababa.

Serneels, P., M. Lindelow, J. Garcia-Montalvo, and A. Barr. 2004. "An Honorable Calling? Findings from the First Wave of a Cohort Study with Final-Year Nursing and Medical Students in Ethiopia." Oxford University, Oxford, United Kingdom.

SNNPR (Southern Nations, Nationalities and Peoples Region). 2005. "Overview of Inter-regional Government Fiscal Relation in the SNNPR." Presentation at the Government of Ethiopia-Donor IGR Workshop, Addis Ababa, March 23.

Suleiman, A. 1995. "Evaluating the Efficiency of Farmers in Ethiopia." *Ethiopian Journal of Economics* 35(2):47–66.

USAID/WLI (U.S. Agency for International Development/World Learning Incorporated) 2004. "Basic Education Strategic Objective 2: Community Government Partnership Program." Annual Report. Washington, D.C.

Weir, S., and J. Knight. 1996. "Household Demand for Schooling (Rural Survey)." PHRD Study 1. Oxford University, Centre for the Study of African Economies, Oxford.

World Bank. 2004a. "Ethiopia: Draft Budget Update, 2004/05." Background note for the 2004 Joint Budget and Aid Review. A World Bank/DBS Joint Assessment, Washington, D.C.

———. 2005a. "Education in Ethiopia: Strengthening the Foundation for Sustainable Progress." Report 28037-ET. Washington, D.C.

———. 2005b. "Ethiopia: A Country Status Report on Health and Poverty." 2 vols. Report 28963-ET, Washington, D.C.

———. 2005c. "Well-Being and Poverty in Ethiopia: The Role of Agriculture and Agency." Report 29468-ET, Washington, D.C.

———. 2005d. "Empowerment in Ethiopia: Issues and Options." Draft. Part of the Ethiopia Institutional Governance Review.

———. 2006a. "Ethiopia: Review of Public Finance." Draft. Washington, D.C.

———. 2006b. "Youth in Africa's Labor Market." Vol. II. Country Case Studies. Washington, D.C.

Eco-Audit

Environmental Benefits Statement

The World Bank is committed to preserving Endangered Forests and natural resources. We print World Bank Working Papers and Country Studies on 100 percent postconsumer recycled paper, processed chlorine free. The World Bank has formally agreed to follow the recommended standards for paper usage set by Green Press Initiative—a nonprofit program supporting publishers in using fiber that is not sourced from Endangered Forests. For more information, visit www.greenpressinitiative.org.

In 2007, the printing of these books on recycled paper saved the following:

Trees*	Solid Waste	Water	Net Greenhouse Gases	Total Energy
264	12,419	96,126	23,289	184 mil.
'40" in height and 6-8" in diameter	Pounds	Gallons	Pounds CO_2 Equivalent	BTUs

green press INITIATIVE